THE HEART IS A SACRED SPACE

PAMELA HAYES

The Heart is a Sacred Space

A Reflection for 2000 AD

ST PAULS

My thanks are due to the following for permission to quote from copyright material: Paulist Press for an extract from *The Pursuit of Wisdom*, 1988. I.C.S. Publications for three extracts from *The Collected Works of St John of the Cross*, 1979. Sheed and Ward Ltd for a passage from Karl Rhaner in *Christian in the Market Place*, 1966. Routledge Ltd for two extracts from C.G. Jung in *The Secret of the Golden Flower*, 1962; and *Collected Works 11*, 1958. Editions du Seuil, Paris for two passages from P. Teilhard de Chardin in *Les Directions de L'Avenir*, 1973; and *Le Coeur de la Matiere*, 1976. Editions Grasset, Paris for two passages from P. Teilhard de Chardin in *Ecrits du Temps de la Guerre*, 1965. E. Mitchell and Addison Wesley Publishing Company for lines from astronauts, in *The Home Planet*, edited by Kevin W. Kelley, 1988. Penguin Books Ltd. for extract from *The Upanishads*, 1965. The Way Publications for use of article by Pamela Hayes: *Women and the Passion* in *The Way Supplement*, Spring 1987. Cathedral Notre Dame de Chartres, 28003 Chartres Cedex for photograph of Chartres interior in *Revue Notre Dame de Chartres. No. 58*, March 1984. Fundacion Coleccion Thyssen – Bornemisza, Madrid for reproduction of Bartolomeo Suardi's Risen Christ. World Perspectives, U.S.A. for NASA image of planet earth.

ST PAULS
Middlegreen, Slough SL3 6BT, United Kingdom
Moyglare Road, Maynooth, Co. Kildare, Ireland

© ST PAULS (UK) 1995

ISBN 085439 493 1

Set by TuKan, High Wycombe
Printed by Redwood Books, Trowbridge

ST PAULS is an activity of the priests and brothers of the Society of St Paul who proclaim the Gospel through the media of social communication

For Jennifer, Claire, Katherine,
and all who hold the future in their heart

Contents

For ease in use, all Biblical references are in the text. Quotations are taken from NRSV. If the author has translated any phrase differently, an asterisk is added to the reference.

Introduction

"The little space within the heart
is as great as this vast universe.
The heavens and the earth are there,
and the sun, and the moon, and the stars;
fire and lightning and winds are there;
and all that now is and all that is not:
for the whole universe is in God
and God dwells within our heart."[1]

This reflection is about discovering "the little space within the heart:" a poetic image suggesting that most intimate reality that seems to hold the key to personal identity and meaning.

Those whom we call mystics claim some experience of this space and attempt to express and explore its existence in images that inevitably remain mysterious even while they attract. But the reality hidden within poetic symbols still seems to fascinate in spite of the overwhelming pressure of everyday living that sometimes stifles efforts to grasp its truth.

In the climate of thought prevailing at the close of the twentieth century the "space within the heart" seems to have the capacity to focus the vision of those who believe in humanity and the world along with those who also believe in God because the space of the heart suggests a sense of belonging and a sense of home.

The claim of the lived experience of faith articulated in this reflection, however, is that the space within the heart reveals not only the core of personal identity but points beyond the source of individual meaning to the ground of all being: an inner centre of connectedness and relationship to which religious tradition has given the name God. In this context awareness of immanence makes known the fact of transcendence: God as the root of our relatedness. God, then, is not simply a God outside and over against creation, analogous to another being, but the sustaining, integrating and loving presence within it, who yet transcends it, by the fact of making it creatively interconnected, interrelated, and therefore, whole. The real truth, for the experience of faith, is that the heart is a sacred space.

Such a claim inevitably has profound implications for the way in which human beings live and relate with each other and take responsibility for planet earth. But lest any attempt is made to polarise categories of people, it is salutary to realise that many who would deny belief in an image of God may be closer to a genuine belief in the reality because of their concern both for human beings and for ecological values. Negative images of God often generated through unkind human experience, may impose a need for a phase of apparent atheism to allow for a cleansing of the doors of perception. But the delicate web of wholeness felt to derive from the heart as the unifying centre of reality, is a cause for hope. For when it is personally discovered that the heart is a sacred space, then the sense of belonging and the sense of home may converge in a sense of God.

Hope intimates that life is the journey through which we could discover this truth of the heart for ourselves. But experience of the negative aspects of human existence both in their global proportions and in individual relationships, however we describe them in terms of evil, suffering or sin, seems to block access to the truth that could liberate for life in all its fullness. Fear of disintegrating forces prevents us from being energised by the life-renewing centre within. Only the experience of unconditional love seems capable of opening up the way to that inner space of the heart.

The purpose of the Jesus story for the human situation is to give a human face to the liberating power of such unconditional love both as a vision of reality that may truthfully be called God, and as creating a possibility of growth that could become personally individuated in any human life.

By giving effective access to the experience of forgiveness, healing and inner freedom, Jesus is that image of God who defuses the fear that paralyses, and so opens us to the energising truth of our own inner space. What is actual in him speaks of what is a God-like possibility for us. Jesus points to the treasure hidden within our own heart.

The image is one that was made real for us when the heart of Jesus was pierced open as he died upon the cross, symbolising the release of the life-giving power of the Spirit of God. This is an image of God that a world aware of its own brokenness can receive because it holds the hope of new life breaking through death whatever its guise. The open heart of the pierced Christ speaks more eloquently than words of a world wounded and yet loved by God. There in the wholeness of an image we see at the heart of human pain the compassion of God's love. Symbolically it proclaims, in prophetic style, human life lived beyond fear, trusting in the power of God's unconditional love, and so prepared to live from that sacred space of the heart in faith, hope and love, as Jesus pioneers the way to its living and life-giving truth.

With this theological vision opening up the way, the possibility is set before us of making an inner journey designed to take us to the space of the heart. Jesus is seen as inviting us first to come and see and then to follow in the pattern of his life, learning all the while from God how to be human.

Aware of the borderland between psychology and spirituality, the creative possibilities of pain as integral to learning how to love, are explored, since they belong to the questions of the heart. But, while finding opportunities for healing at every level of growth, the thrust of the journey is towards personal availability for life.

Discovering the sacred space of the heart inevitably ensures a return from that inner centre of wisdom to some form of prophetic involvement in the adventure of creation. To come close to God means to catch fire and be impelled towards a mission of compassion. This is love's justice for a planet in need of healing and nurture to a maturity that is God's dream for the earth. Only God's kind of loving for all humankind can manifest the cosmic radiance of the sacred space of the heart.

While the modern approach to biblical exegesis, as opposed to a literal fundamentalism, is fully accepted in this reflection, the Scriptures are used for this journey according to the contemplative tradition of Christian spirituality. This has meant allowing the text to speak to our condition now, without necessarily placing it within its historical context. For in this case the word of God in Scripture, acting as an objective light, is there to facilitate the discovery of our uniquely personal way as we reflect upon the Spirit's guidance in our own experience.

This interaction is encouraged and shaped by the dynamic at work in *The Spiritual Exercises* of Ignatius of Loyola which gives the whole process its discerning quality and apostolic thrust. At the heart of the dynamic is a freedom movement: a freedom *from* all that could hinder growth to full maturity in Christ; and a freedom *for* all that God wants to achieve in and through us. Each pilgrim is given the means to find their own personal calling as a way of sharing in the global outreach of Christ's mission.

There are, however, differences of emphasis and image from the original Ignatian ground-plan. These stem from a feminine or anima vantage point alive in the spiralling process adopted as a method of proceeding. Moving to and from the heart centre of the pilgrimage implies rounding off the edges separating one phase from another. But anyone familiar with the ground-plan will recognise characteristic landmarks under their Scriptural disguise as well as the Ignatian principle of adaptation at work.

The spiralling process adopted as particularly appropriate for a pilgrimage to the heart is explained in the Prologue. The inspiration derives from two mandalas imaged in Chartres Cathedral: the great west rose window and the labyrinth on the pavement below it. They provide both a vision and a map for the pilgrimage to the heart, as to the centre of a mandala. This pilgrimage is illuminated and lived by Jesus before we are invited to make the journey.

At the end of the pilgrimage we return, in the Epilogue, to the concept of the mandala as to that image capable of containing both the vision and the pilgrim's progress towards it, only now we are offered an opportunity of creating a new cosmic mandala for the sacred space of the heart.

The style adopted throughout the reflection includes sub-headings, scriptural texts and poetic lines breaking up the chapters into short sections. This is deliberate since they act as pace-maker, slowing down the process so as to encourage personal reflection. For it belongs to the poetic word to awaken us to the paradox and beauty of truth, as it belongs to the prophetic word to urge us to act from its power. But, as the circular image of the mandala suggests, the work is best seen as a whole. Like a web of fragile threads of meaning, it gains in clarity from the links created and their convergence upon the centre. For the connecting links demonstrate that ultimately the truth that gives healing must bear fruit in compassion for the most vulnerable, and that the wisdom and power that make this possible derive from an awareness of the creative and loving presence of God in our own heart. The psychotherapy of the healer, the spirituality of the mystic and the social justice of the prophet can never be isolated concerns but only related aspects of a holistic appreciation of life.

The work is written from the standpoint of one who has found meaning within the Christian tradition but in a context that is appreciative of the contribution of other world religions and enlightened humanism to the common search for meaning. It is simply personal reflection but it obviously owes more than can ever be adequately acknowledged to the scholarship and teaching of others.

The writing has emerged out of a long oral tradition of talks open to the energising presence of very varied groups of people. They have enabled its articulation, refined it, shaped it, and stretched its possibilities. Inevitably the writing does not convey the animation of the live experience which adapts to particular situations at specific times. But these pages are written with such people in mind and as a token of gratitude for all who have shared their lives and reflecting with me over the years. I have learnt and continue to learn everything from such experience.

Many of these people belong to the Christian tradition and want to make their own what they have glimpsed of the adventure of the spirit as integral to human life. Others have gained spiritual insights from another world religion and want to integrate them into a familiar context of belief. Some have explored the more individual path of depth psychology and want to relate it to the contemplative way trailed by the mystics. All are involved in helping others: some as spiritual guides, others in a variety of ways. They represent all who are open to the deepest and widest concerns of the human heart in search of meaning and want a life both deeply centred in spiritual values and fully inserted in the needs and pressures of contemporary society. The hope is that in sharing this reflection they may be encouraged in their ministry, especially to those who will not be helped by the pages of a book but only by a personal encounter with someone fully alive to the sacred space of the heart.

It is impossible to thank by name all those who have encouraged me to write, but Winifred Rushforth O.B.E., Francis Gresham O.P., James Walsh S.J. and Joseph Warrilow O.S.B. will always remain alive in a grateful memory. I also wish to thank Bill Broderick S.J. for asking me to write a paper for the Spiritual Exercises conference at St Beuno's, North Wales, on *Women and the Passion* which was later published in *The Way Supplement* no. 58, Spring 1987. It gave me the opportunity of articulating ideas that are given space in this reflection.

I am grateful, too, for a threefold support that bears the mark of Switzerland. Andrée Meylan R.S.C.J. launched me in the task of writing. Janine Koutchoumow kept me writing and suggested publication and the Baron Heinrich Thyssen-Bornemisza very kindly invited me to see the original of Bartolomeo Suardi's Risen Christ, housed at that time in the Villa Favorita, Lugano, Switzerland. The painting's challenge to faith seemed to haunt me until I began to write. Now I am able to record my gratitude to the Thyssen-Bornemisza Foundation for permission to reproduce a copy of this masterpiece.

Sincere thanks are also due to Janet Elliott for her careful typing of the first long draft and to Freda Parkinson R.S.C.J. not only for her creative photography but also for her patient hard work and attention to detail with the word processor to bring the work to completion. I also want to thank Edward Yarnold S.J. for kindly reading through the completed manuscript and making several helpful suggestions, and Vincent Siletti and the staff of St Pauls for their encouragement and care over its publication.

Finally, I would like to thank the world-wide religious community of the Society of the Sacred Heart to which I belong, for a living spirit I tend to take for granted. In particular, I want to thank Helen McLaughlin and, since the list would be too long if I started to name individuals, all the members of the Society in the United Kingdom, especially my own Woldingham community, for their continuous support.

Clearly, the writing remains unfinished business. Reflection is for life and living. We each have to earth our vision in a life-style that is uniquely our own. But for all of us who, on the threshold of a new millennium, still dare to believe and hope and love, a prophetic word proclaimed centuries before Christ echoes clearly,

> "Comfort my people. Speak to the heart.
> Lift up your voice. Do not be afraid,
> and say, 'Here is your God!'"

(Isaiah 40:1,9*)

For God has made a home in the space of our heart.

Pilgrimage
To the Heart:
A Reflection
on the Rose Window
and the Labyrinth in
Chartres
Cathedral

1

Prologue:
A Pilgrimage to the Heart

1.1 Chartres: the Rose Window and the Labyrinth

This journey begins with Chartres
that hollowed out and hallowed in
sacred space:
gem of beauty dedicated to the Virgin Mother
hollowed out and hallowed in
with God, her son.

Enter this holy place and see!
Let deep stirrings awake
that restlessness of soul seeking God.
Then sit and look at this majesty,
passive, open to its power,
drawing now from within.

This journey is a pilgrimage:
extended prayer in time and space,
a seeking and a finding of God,
a pilgrim's way to the heart,
the home centre within and beyond.
Enter this inner space and be still.

A quality of darkness, heavy in stone,
receiving inconceivable richness of light.
Through glass, stained with multi-tinted hue:
golden flame, wine red and clarity of blue,
is light, dancing, glancing,
creating a vision: a rose window.

Light streams: a shaft of radiant beams
encircled by the gloom.
Now an explosion of colour,
then a tranquil glowing circle of reconciliation
suspended between floor and vault,
hovering between earth and heaven.

A rose cut jewel: transparent
window onto a transcendent world;
a call to something beyond,
showing one thing, inviting to another.
There in the rose, deepening as it spirals,
is the pilgrim's way, homing towards its centre.

A cruciform tension inlays the circle,
wheel of life moving between dark and light,
psychic struggle between unconscious good
    and evil,
balancing four energies, qualities of
    consciousness:
thought and feeling, sensing and intuition;
until the radial paths become radiant.

Flamboyant imaging:
a mandala of cosmic wholeness
reconciling all creation in a union of love;
living flames of wisdom's spirit
tonguing forth the word,
Christ, the sacred heart.

Yet this vision of future glory:
healing mandala,
our dreams' pattern of order,
cosmic and psychic wholeness,
transforming matter in spirit,
awaits a time process for realisation.

What is seen in symbol cannot be imparted in
    words
  but must be realised in living.
Labyrinthine is the way, in and out,
composed of trial and error,
learnt in patience, slowly, step by step,
persevering in space and time.

One path through concentric circles,
the Spirit guiding through discernment and
    reflection
to the centre of truth:
a wound of knowing, a wisdom of loving;
returning the same way, wiser in love's knowing,
to the reality of life at the circle's edge.

So is the rose mandala,
window of meaning,
superimposed
on the earthed labyrinth:
light projected onto life,
centred and radiant.

1.2 The Concept of the Mandala

The west rose window and the labyrinth on the pavement in Chartres cathedral are two interrelated mandalas.
They hold in tension a vision of the pilgrim's journey to the
heart and the living out of that journey in a spirit of pilgrimage. This is a creative tension because the hope is that
what is symbolised by these two mandalas should somehow be integrated, so that the vision becomes a lived reality of wholeness. The tension persists until the vision is
earthed: the west rose window illuminating the labyrinthine pilgrim way until the reality is imaged in one mandala.
Carl Jung was one of the western pioneers in relating
the idea of the mandala as a therapeutic device to the

eastern concept of the mandala as an aid to meditation. He outlined its value as a basic tool for personal growth and spiritual enrichment open to every human being in search of meaning.[2]

'Mandala' is the Sanskrit word for circle, the symbol of the cosmos in its entirety. But the universality of the mandala lies in its one constant: the principle of the centre, the source of all creative energy. In the centre all is one and whether it is manifested in a star, a rose or a human being, the same centre is its heart. In it we may discover our cosmic communion in a present moment of awareness.

A mandala normally consists of a series of concentric circles suggesting a path between different dimensions to the centre. There are innumerable variants on the motif, but they tend to be based on some form of squaring of the circle by means of a cruciform shape intersecting its centre. The basic motif is the premonition of a centre of the personality, a kind of central point within the psyche, which is a source of energy to which everything is related and by which everything is arranged. The energy of the centre point is manifested in the natural urge to live out the potential of our whole personality.

The mandala is meant to help concentration by narrowing down the psychic field of vision to the centre. This is intended to facilitate both a deeper level of integration and a higher level of awareness. By concentrating energy, an organism can heal itself, grow and expand beyond itself.

Healing, growth and becoming centred belong to the basic twofold rhythm of the mandala process. There is the movement of birth from the centre towards a world of creative differentiation. Then there is the return movement from the circle towards the unity of the centre and the potential of new life. Human consciousness is defined by the polarity of this contrasting rhythm, and conversion at every level is to be seen in the turning full circle that belongs to the spiralling process of the mandala.

The mandala begins with a visualisation that leads to a realisation of the source of energy within. It ends by releasing that energy, to the extent that the person concentrating upon it is capable of identifying with it. This is possible because the mandala is a kind of cosmic image of the underlying pattern of wholeness provided by the web of life that supports and sustains us. It contains the energy from the unconscious in a form that can be assimilated by consciousness. The circle draws a protective line around our physical and psychological space so that our identity can emerge as we find a focus for the concentration of our energy. This has a calming effect, inviting the conflicting parts of our nature to surface. In this way the release of tension is facilitated as opposites are accepted and reconciled. Crises can then be seen for what they are: normal aspects of the living process, defining, in fact, junctures of growth. In practice, healing and growth really have meaning only as responses to those crises which every human being encounters. In this way the mandala becomes a symbol of the liberation that is its purpose.

When we create a mandala we cultivate a relationship with our energy creating centre which is essential for our healing and growth into wholeness. A fully individuated human being is able to maintain contact with its centre, and to assimilate all experience without losing touch with the vital source within, no matter what may happen outwardly. This is personal integration.

1.3 The Process in the Pilgrimage

A pilgrimage to the heart takes on the process of the mandala as it both centres and radiates. The dynamic involves a spiralling back and forth from the circle of life where we are fully involved, to the centre which gives it meaning. Through such a movement the creative multi–plicity of human and cosmic experience is centred in a spiritual unity that is its heart.

The heart symbol remains a constant reminder of the necessity of always moving towards the centre. To lay hold upon that which is essential is its primary concern. From this centre we are enabled to return to the circle of everyday life with a new personal vision and the energy to live by it. This happens by means of the uniquely human process of reflection which values repetition in the sense of returning to moments of personal significance in order to deepen their impact and so facilitate growth. This means constantly, in some sense, returning to the place where we started and knowing it as if for the first time. We re-cover familiar ground by remembering previous experience, but with a new perception gained through fresh experience and the distancing perspective of hindsight. Such an exercise rests surely on the truth that we shall always need to begin again, realizing that even when we have gained some real maturity, we shall know in our heart that we are beginners still and accept our learners status graciously and gladly.

Such a spiralling process remains ever mindful of the values of wholeness and reverence for life, gathering and gleaning truth from wherever it may be found. It suggests readily and fearlessly moving out into an involvement with the world as an important adventure necessary for holistic human growth. It means a kind of hovering above and about every new experience, rather like a helicopter negotiating a delicate task. It asks for a feeling into a situation, so that it is not merely known conceptually, but experientially, from the inside, with a measure of immediacy that can lead to conversion of life. Quite literally, the process circles round its centre of interest in order to grasp its measure from different vantage points. But it also points to a homing in to a centre of significance as it reaches the core of truth.

The symbol of the heart, therefore, emphasises two things: attaining to the truth that is essential; and the inclusion of many distinctive facets which point the way to what is essential. These are not the same thing, and yet there is a significant overlap. An approach to the four Gospels of the New Testament provides an apt illustration. The essential message of the Christian Gospel may be gleaned from any one of the four Gospels. But the way in which that message is expressed will provide what is distinctive in each particular Gospel. It is precisely this combination of what is essential with what is distinctive that gives this spiral process its particular value.

It is art that provides us with what is distinctive in modes of expression and so takes us into the manifold values symbolised by the heart: values of feeling and human warmth, values of attraction and inspiration, values of creativity and communication. These sometimes seem to move away from what is essential, but in the world of education and communication it is precisely through what is distinctive in various forms of art that we find the power that can attract towards what is essential and make it manifest and appealing. In a world, therefore, of many facets and manifold cultures and personalities, the important thing is to know how to penetrate any creative and particular manifestation to its central core, while respecting the multiformity of the outer layers that both earth the essential reality and make it accessible to further human experience. The message is not the method of communication, but it depends so much upon the method for its effective communication. The heart speaks of the centre point of all reality: unrefracted and unreflected truth. But it also speaks of reflected truth: its radiance in creation and creativity.

1.4 The Heart: A sign for the Times

"The real character of a particular age is not on the whole what is most familiar but what is denied and yet ordained. What could this possibly be today, if not the need and the task of rediscovering the heart, and of bearing the burden of our own hearts: their loneliness, their night of unhappiness and their anxiety at the thought of God."[3]

Understanding something of the process of the pilgrimage is relevant not only if we are to arrive, but also if we are to grow through the experience. But the journey's end is what gives it meaning and purpose. Our journey is a pilgrimage to the heart.

The search for the heart must be true of every age, since it belongs to being human, but it is a characteristic of our time that many have not yet found their own heart. We are aware of an ever increasing number of people living without meaning and purpose, lacking a sense of personal identity that discovers their uniqueness. The situation is aggravated by a certain type of technological rationalism that removes the intellect from the humanising influence of personal feeling. A kind of outer shell of cynicism seems to muzzle any spontaneous inner response. Meanwhile, the emotions, bereft of the mind's direction, become largely chaotic instead of being harnessed for meaningful commitment. Yet the desire to know by experience something felt to lie beyond the immediacy of the senses, remains hidden in the depths of each person. The evidence is there for all to see, in the prevailing interest in meditation techniques and gurus of every kind, as well as in the mystical dimension of religion in both East and West, along with the upsurge of longing for the spiritual that characterises so many of the New Age movements.

The real paradox of our times lies in the fact that there is no effective recognition of the need for an integrating and unifying centre, pointing both within and beyond, as being essential to the personality if it is to become truly human. Spiritual yearnings crest the waves of human desire but the ebbing tides so often reveal murky waters of materialism run riot in lust and greed. It seems as though a human hand lashes about in the raging sea of experience grasping at anything suggestive of life, heedless of the fact that the clue to life's meaning lies in the very buoyancy of the ocean itself. Anxious and ambitious, it reaches out, struggling to achieve, but it has not the courage to let go and trust to the flow of the tide and the power that lies both within and beyond itself in the symbol of the ocean. Many who, theoretically, do not believe in God, have, in practice, made their own god, and inevitably suffer from a certain de-energising frustration in having nothing beyond themselves to awaken that which lies within. The modern world may claim a certain understanding of what is generally expressed in the term 'heart'. But the full reality of what is symbolised seems to elude the experience of those who have no centre calling them forth for a purpose beyond themselves. Nothing portrays this lack and emptiness so well as the Henry Moore sculptures with figures circumscribing a void circular shape in the place where the heart would be. They cry out for a response of the heart that would appear to be a sign for the times. But what do we really mean by the term 'heart'?

1.5 Rediscovering the Heart

After centuries of cultural use in many languages, the term 'heart' remains a primary word, rich and multi-faceted in meaning. Its popular graphic use, with an arrow piercing the heart, has lasted through many generations as easily understood shorthand expressing human love. But the popular and ordinary use of the term 'heart' extends more widely in its outreach.

The word 'heart' is both more complex and more inclusive in its simplicity than any attempt to define it. There is a sense in which it touches every aspect of the human personality. The biological use of the word by no means exhausts its meaning but already points to obvious metaphorical use. The pounding of the heartbeat and the circulation of the blood to and from the heart, together with the rhythm of breathing, suggest an inward and outward flow as inherent to the dynamic of every human life in its growth towards wholeness. The heart is the centre of a natural mandala.

As the source of life and energy, however, it is natural

that the heart should have become the symbolic focus of love and affection along with the creativity they engender. Life erupts and exhilarates in deep feeling and passion, and dances with desire as the quickening pulse affirms. It becomes warm and tender in compassion as love creates a web of relatedness both personal and cosmic. The heart in this mode is radiant and expansive.

The heart, however, also transforms the way in which we know. When the intellect acts as the processor of knowledge, it tends to differentiate and polarise, in order to clarify its concepts. This gives vital access to the light of reason. But there is a knowing of the heart that we call wisdom, in which intuition reconciles seeming opposites to enable a more unified and holistic grasp of truth. In this process the memory is so stirred by the imagination that the heart distils the discourse of the mind in a moment of insight. The heart then functions in favour of a process of discernment that can be harnessed for effective choice and true commitment precisely because it is more whole. Decisions implemented in this way ensure that life can really be lived, as the feelings of human beings are protected as well as the values of truth that guide the mind.

As discernment moves into decision for a lifestyle, however, we are reminded that the heart also points to the moral quality of human action and intention. Generosity implies wholeheartedness in action as sincerity speaks of truth and the genuine character of the heart's intentions. Fidelity meanwhile touches upon the heart's steadfast and abiding love that is the harbinger of trust. But it is surely courage that most readily bears witness to the values of the heart in choices that open out into the kind of commitment that can transform a human life.

From ordinary use, therefore, the heart appears as the source of an experience which lies somewhere between gut reaction and cerebral knowing. It is analogous to intuition, involving deep feeling and moral values but it transcends and integrates all such experience in the depth and wholeness of its response. Such a breadth of ordinary usage that moves easily from the physical to the symbolic, points to the heart as the deepest core of the human personality where we are most essentially ourselves and so find our unique identity and meaning.

Beyond all this, however, the heart is the centre of unity: the innermost spiritual reality unifying all experience. It is the sacred space in which the mystery of human personality opens onto the mystery of God. It is an inner flame giving light and warmth: the witness to a presence generating spiritual power and energy.

Such a capacity to bear so much richness in an integrated and holistic way makes the word 'heart' irreplaceable and so, in the last analysis, a genuine primordial symbol. It needs to be rediscovered as we cross the threshold of a new millennium.

2.

A World Wounded Yet Loved by God

2.1 The Truth that Sets us Free

The mandala of the rose window in Chartres Cathedral remains only a symbol pointing to a process that has to be lived. It is like a map, but it is not the journey. It is to this life pilgrimage that we must now turn.

There is a restlessness in every human being that wants to go beyond the outer trappings of what it knows, to penetrate the shell of life and taste the kernel at its heart. Standing at the circle edge of life's mandala, involved in its everyday events, we are yet fascinated and drawn by the pull of its centre. Our deepest desire is for the truth that will set us free to be ourselves and we sense that somehow in that centre we can find the self-authenticating truth that will give meaning to life. To go in search of this treasure buried in our own heart seems to be the adventure to which life calls us.

The echo of this call lingers with us to motivate our setting out, but we are hampered by an image of ourselves and our world derived from our everyday life. For what we actually experience in our human situation is so much meaninglessness and fragmentation, both individually and collectively. We may call this sin, self-alienation, soul-sickness or brokenness. But we are aware of a deep wound at the centre of our personality dividing us within ourselves and from each other. The centre that draws us appears to be wounded: the heart seems literally to be broken.

Such awareness gives rise to feelings of guilt and worth-lessness, generating unresolved fear and self doubt that are actually more harmful to us than the moral failures that erupt from such a seed bed. This depressed state is aggravated by the fact that instead of recognising the frustration with ourselves as a reaction to our own frequent faults and failings, we project our anger on to others including God, whose existence we may still question.

The unkind behaviour that continues to arise out of the depths of such woundedness only succeeds in hurting us still more and making us more hurtful to others. Yet with all such experience of the human situation we remain convinced that the release of energy for a meaningful life does depend upon our genuine identity being known and accepted. Only the truth can set us free.

2.2 Psychology and the Shadowland of Truth

Human beings can still make or mar our world so it is significant, at this point in time, that evolution seems to be focussed on the yet undiscovered or unrealised potential of the human psyche. Human capacity for reflection, for folding back upon itself, in its thought, its feeling and its very consciousness, has created a new perspective in human knowing. The age-long challenge to know ourselves has found sharper instruments for probing in the findings of depth psychology. Along with all its variants in psychotherapy, it operates both for healing and for understanding the human psyche. Appreciating the power of unconscious influences in the determination of our conscious actions, it is concerned to liberate the psyche both for personal growth and interpersonal relationships. Such a journey towards wholeness is seen in terms of an ever deeper penetration into the depths of the psyche so that every facet is recognised, accepted and progressively integrated at a new level of consciousness. The dynamic is at once a process of interiorisation and unification which is of the essence of becoming a person.

The theory is clear but the practice is not easy. The reconciling of opposites within ourselves does imply accepting to know them by allowing our unconscious world to become conscious. But meeting our shadow self can be painful. We realise just how vulnerable we are when we learn of our hidden motivations and inner compulsions. Our pain is compounded when we see that the violence we so deplore and project on to others lurks in the dark recesses of our own unconscious. But such vulnerability belongs to a sincere striving for our own truth and contains a long lesson in becoming a person. At each level of our growth we are invited to let go our inherent resistance and to take back the projections that mirror our shadow self so that more and more of what we saw as other and outside our self may be integrated into our own person.

The challenge is to stay with our woundedness and the limiting flaws in our make-up. For the wounds of each one of us are those areas of deep psychic sensitivity which provide the point of entry into our heart. It is through the very enduring itself that we can come to that deep centre within upon which depends the authenticity of our lives. Total acceptance of our humanity and of the human condition is the only way to emerge through brokenness to a wholeness that discovers the meaning of life. If we dare to face what it means to be fully human with all its fragility, the word of truth pierces us in the innermost depths of our experience and sets us free. The wounded heart is in reality the most realistic symbol of the new unitive centre emerging as the reconciler of opposites in the human person.

2.3 The Love that Casts Out Fear

Notionally, we are likely to be convinced that the truth can set us free, and to endorse the process suggested by psychology. But rarely does any process designed for self-knowledge achieve by itself such a goal. Even the most robust psyche cannot bear too much truth. We are afraid of the shadow within ourselves even more than a child can be afraid of a shadow cast by a glimmer of light in the dark.

We need the security of love before we can venture far into the quest for personal truth. Only the caring warmth and understanding support of love can provide a safe foundation for growth into the truth that is both living and liberating. From the first moment of conception we need to be wanted, cherished and nurtured in love so that we have a reasonable chance of becoming genuinely mature adults, unafraid to be ourselves. If we feel secure in love we shall be able at each phase of our lives to let go of what we are, in favour of what we could become. Instead of clinging in fear to what we think we possess, we shall have open hands, free to take the ongoing gift of life that comes to us as our own unique truth.

Human love can achieve this creative task and fundamental therapy. But it remains frail and fragile; and experience tells us that we cannot always be sure of it. Many seem to be deprived of such love even in their earliest years. All of us meet with its instability and limitations. Still, there remains the human need for a love that is constant and in which we can trust completely, regardless of what life holds. Such unconditional love is the name for God: the love that casts out fear, because ultimately it challenges our limited conception of the truth, and so can and will set us free.

2.4 Theology and the Light of Truth

Our journey began with an awareness of the human situation as one of alienation from ourselves and one another. This was because it is an obvious part of our daily experience. But what we do not easily recognise is that its root lies in a practical alienation from God.

The consequences of such a view of reality are more serious than we imagine. We are under the illusion that we can arrive at a true knowledge of ourselves apart from God. This is not in any way to deny the value of psychology as an aid to effective self knowledge. Our consciousness and personal responsibility are enhanced by its discoveries. But without an experience of the healing power of love which gives unique value to each person, fear and self-doubt may only increase as the negative aspects of the psyche are encountered. Awareness of our wounds tends to make us close up and turn in upon ourselves rather than open up for healing. We are afraid because we sense that inevitably we shall be led into those painful shadowlands of truth which have already made us so vulnerable. We may know that we need to acknowledge our wounds and that acceptance is part of the process of healing. But we need to be taken beyond fear and to know that the anguish inherent in human fragility is not the whole truth. The wounded heart is not only a psychological symbol of human vulnerability. It is also a powerful symbol of a theological reality.

Fear of confronting the deviousness within the human heart has the effect of cutting us off from the creative source of energy within. Turning from our deepest self means, in effect, turning from God within us. Our essential relatedness to God constitutes the root of our being, grounded in God. Such is the mystery of the human heart. We are created in the image of God with an orientation to God in our inmost self. We are, therefore, necessarily disorientated until this God is the focus of our whole life, integrating the humanity we experience every day with the essential ground of our being, which is God's image in us. The truth is that we cannot truly know ourselves apart from the love and affirmation of God. We are often in danger of equating humanity with what we know of the negative aspects of human existence. God sees humanity with compassion and knows us with all the creative potential of love.

Cosmic and human history attempt to make this love of God known in the complex beauty of creation and the truth of human growth and creativity in spite of all its failures. The same truth is repeated in many different ways but the work of God is consistent despite what we may think are appearances to the contrary.

"Do not fear, for I have redeemed you;
I have called you by your name, you are mine.
When you pass through the waters, I will be with
    you.
When you walk through fire, you shall not be
    burned.
For I am the Lord, your God, your Saviour.
You are precious in my sight
    and honoured, and I love you."

(Isaiah 43:1-4)

"Does a woman forget her baby at the breast,
or fail to cherish the son of her womb?
Even these may forget, yet I will not forget you.
See, I have inscribed you on the palms of my
    hands."

(Isaiah 49: 15-16)

Fear of the shadowland of psychological truth could
prevent us from seeing the light of the theological truth that
God loves us in our woundedness with a love that is steadfast and enduring. In shadow and in light, God remains the
very ground of our being and the source of our life.

The clarity of psychological truth sharpens our perception of the deviance present in the human psyche along
with all its creative possibilities. It helps us to understand
what we have experienced of the woundedness of our
world so that we can be healed. But belief in God offers us
a theological view of reality that takes on board all the evil
of sin and suffering. It is God's own view of a world
wounded and yet loved by God. Such a view enables us to
accept the whole truth that sets us free because it holds us
in the love that casts out fear and creates hope.

2.5 A Hug: An Image of God's Prodigal Love

There is a homely scene which can image our prior need
for love if we are to face the truth about ourselves. A good

37

mother does not spank a tired and fractious child. She picks the little one up and gives him a hug. Later there might be some talking about the behaviour. But first comes the hug. Surprising though it may seem, this is how God treats each one of us. The authority for such a conviction comes from a story in the Christian tradition that is rightly famous. It tells us so much about God and ourselves that we need a pause to reflect on it (Luke 15:11-32).

The story is about a father and his two sons. The younger, having asked for his share of the family inheritance, goes off and squanders it in riotous living until he is reduced to utter dependence for survival. This apparent mid-life crisis has the effect of confronting him with some home truths. Having lost all that he had, he is suddenly brought face to face with himself. He literally "came to himself." His motives for deciding to change direction were not all to do with recognising the selfishness of his life so far. He was hungry. He did, however, begin by making a choice, although the choice appeared to be forced upon him by the direness of the circumstances. He could not do anything else. Still, the younger son's words suggested genuine sorrow for the past and a readiness to begin again with a return journey to his Father in a spirit of repentance. This was a real turning point: conversion.

"I will get up and go to my Father
and I will say to him, 'Father,
I have sinned against heaven and before you.
I am no longer worthy to be called your son.'"
(Luke 15:18-19)

The image of the father suggests only love that waits with longing for the return of a wayward son. Even while the son was a long way off, the father, moved with compassion, ran to embrace him with a warm hug. There was no time for the son to complete his rehearsed speech of repentance because the father was not interested in what had happened in the past He was only concerned about celebrating the present homecoming of a son whom he had thought lost and the future of a new beginning.

Certainly we are intended to see in so loving and forgiving a father, a true image of the generosity and tenderness of God. The enfolding embrace of God is boundless: simply the climax of an ever waiting love looking from afar off for our return, however inhuman or degrading our behaviour.

We need such an image to focus our minds because images mediate between the conscious and the unconscious, to release the flow of energy. So many of our images of God stifle and block the flow of life because they are the projection on to God, as a powerful figure, of painful or downright harmful experiences of relationship in our early, impressionable years. Dominating authority exercised without love or respect, engenders feelings of resentment and anger or furthers the introjection of feelings of inadequacy, shame or guilt where they are inappropriate to actual behaviour. Only right images of God enable us to accept the liberating power of truth. This story of the prodigal love of God cleanses the doors of our perception with an image of God, in whose image we are created, so that we in our turn, may love.

The story, however, did not end there. The life of the elder son had not taken on the lustful or wasteful aspects that characterised the life of the younger son. Staying at home working to support his father, he had led what most people would call a good life. But his reaction to his father's celebration of the younger son's return suggested another side to his character. He was unable to rejoice at the return of his younger brother who had ruined his life. He even referred to his brother when speaking to his father, as 'this son of yours' (Luke 15:30).

Jealousy and resentment were clearly present but no compassion or joy at the return of a lost one. In short, there was no understanding of the measure and pain of lostness. It would take some time before his father's reassuring and appreciative words would find a home in his heart.

"Son, you are always with me
and all that is mine is yours.
But we had to celebrate and rejoice, because
this brother of yours was dead and has come to life
he was lost and has been found."

(Luke 15:31-32)

No less than the younger son, this character type of the elder son would also need the assurance of love before facing the truth of his own closed heart, so that he could be liberated for a generosity as universal as that of the prodigal image of God.

What the story of the two sons' life journey does, is allow us to see not only the image of God in the father, but also the image of our many-faceted selves and our shadow, in both the older and the younger son. We can see how the faults and the failings of both the apparently good and the obviously bad can be present in each of us, and how we need to own our projections. Each one of us needs to come to our true self, and to arise and make the re-turn journey, acknowledging our capacity for sin and selfishness, as well as our petty pride and self-righteousness, over against every other human being close to us in our shared humanity and so loved by our creator God. But this can only be done in an awareness of God's love. So in the end the story is about a homecoming to love as all such moments of re-turning to God must be. For it is the image of God that prevails: an image that is to be reflected in both sons, and in all the sons and daughters of God. This is the image of steadfast and tender love that knows what it means to stand in the space of the other: a quality of mercy that is not strained, but simple graciousness that creates hope in life.

The parable, however, has a sequel in a true life story. In this case the elder son, Jesus, is all that the father is in generous love, but he takes upon himself the consequences of the human story of the younger son, who now represents each one of us. In the heart of Jesus is the meeting point of

God and humanity. He is the human face of God. To him we must now turn, for only in Jesus can we really see how our humanity is loved by God.

2.6 God in the Heart of Christ

Modern theology insists that we must begin with the facts about the world's suffering if we want to speak with any relevance about God. But this is only half the truth. The other half has to do with the personally experienced love of God. But when these two truths are brought together we have a source of insight both about God and ourselves that can transform human life and have cosmic repercussions. This is precisely the reconciling process that God has adopted in Jesus through what Christianity calls the mystery of the Incarnation.

The Incarnation is the truth about the God who not only energises the evolving matter of the universe in all its cosmic immensity, but who graciously chooses to take on a human face. It accepts the wonder of the universe and manifests the incomparable value of the human person. But in a creativity that transcends human capacity, it assumes responsibility for the suffering and violence that has erupted into the world. It is founded on the paradox implied not only in the union of matter and spirit, but also in the mystery of God and humanity, united in the person of Jesus: the supreme example of the reconciliation of opposites. For in Jesus, our human nature is personally and wholly united to God, so that the integration of the human and the divine is fully actual. This means that in the pierced heart of Jesus crucified, we see imaged a world wounded and yet loved by God. For there we can see, all at once, the anguish of the world in suffering humanity and the compassion of God loving us towards the wholeness of being human. Here is the whole truth of our humanity and our hope. But we need to unpack so buried a treasure to discover what such godly freedom means within human limits because it is Jesus who gives us the word of truth and freedom (John 8:32,36).

"You will know the truth
and the truth will make you free.
So if the Son makes you free,
you will be free indeed."

2.7 The Jesus Story: Human Limitations

To be real, incarnation must have its initiation point in the here and now, the specific and particular, with all the limitations of time and space that this presupposes. The Jesus story has everything of particularity about it. Jesus, born of a Jewish woman, Mary, in first century Palestine, is the name of this human face in which God manifested himself most personally and effectively for human need. Being born at a particular time and place meant that God allowed himself to be limited by the laws of birth, growth, diminishment and death, as a way of making himself known.

Colourful flowers dotted on green hill-sides and squalling storms on Lake Galilee contrasting with the surrounding arid desert were part of the geographical scene that formed Jesus, nurtured in a Palestine bridging the Mediterranean world and the Middle East. In the same way the language and culture of the Graeco-Roman world, together with the religion and mentality of the Hebrew Scriptures educated him, at least informally, so that he could cope with a language of paradox in his attempt to articulate something that was inevitably new.

God was now made known within the day to day process of growth, in the detailed happenings of a human life. The human condition was the place of revelation. If God had pitched his tent among us in the desert of this world, as the Aramaic mentality attempted to express this truth, the tent was nothing more or less than human skin.

The revelation was both painfully and wonderfully obvious, so obvious that the simple truth could be missed or avoided. It would need eyes of faith, eyes fully awake to see what could be seen, and ears to hear the word expressed in a humanity so unusually alive to its particular situation.

Still the fact remains, seeing and knowing God entails looking at the person of Jesus, listening to his teaching, understanding him in his relationship with men and women: both the disciples who loved him and those who sought to destroy him, as well as the crowds who thronged about him and the sick who wanted to touch him. It means pondering on the frugality and simplicity of his early years in an unimportant northern village of Galilee as well as following him in his adult ministry as a powerful itinerant preacher and compassionate healer with no fixed abode. But it also means being captured by his vision of God as his Father whose will was everything to him, so much so that his nights would frequently be spent silently alone with that God and the dawn find him in a desert spot where divine love could energise him for his mission.

2.8 At the Crossroad: Suffering Explored

Incarnation, however, does not only mean labour and service but includes suffering and ultimately death. It is at this point that we come quite literally to the crossroad in the life of Jesus.

In no way do the writers of the New Testament Scriptures underestimate the gruesome nature of the death of Jesus, but their purpose is less to consider the detailed process of the death, than to discover the meaning that lies both within and beyond it and in the journey towards it. What signifies clearly in this death is the personal quality of the choices and the commitment to a life-style that led Jesus to this most passive of human experiences, and its character as an unconditional act of love both for God and humanity. For the ultimate fulfilment of the mystery of the Incarnation is allowed by God to depend upon human freedom and the consequences of such a gift: the problem of evil, sin and the whole panorama of what is considered negative in the human condition.

It was this sinful and suffering human condition that God made personally his own in taking on the humanity of Jesus. What we need to absorb is the fact that Jesus began by accepting humanity as it was and not as it should be. To reduce this fact in any way, is to deny something essential to the whole mystery of the Incarnation, and so to block the way to human liberation. When we reflect upon our human condition we are content to appreciate all that it brings us of joy, excitement and adventure, but pain, injustice and cruelty create endless questions which turn human aggression outwards in an attempt to change the situation and deal with the problems from the outside. Rarely does any human being choose to enter into the midst of a negative or painful situation, to experience its effects from within and work out a way of liberation from that inner point.

Choosing to plunge in at the deep end of human involvement, to enter into the heart of the matter, finds most human beings reluctant. Fear grips at the human heart, and it dare not believe in the power of human powerlessness. To accept woundedness, let alone choose it, goes against all natural instincts for survival, especially if the name of the game is changing the world, even an infinitesimal part of it. This remains true even though, theoretically, we are prepared to expatiate on the need for empathy when dealing with each others problems, and stress the importance of grass roots experience and getting inside the skin of any situation before attempting to change it. In all this we somehow meet the extraordinary paradox that vitiates the authenticity of our lives, in that we do not really practise what we preach.

2.9 Rebuilding with a Wounded World

Intuitively we grasp the truth that it is essential to penetrate to the heart of any question in order to explore its potential from the inside. Yet there remains the recurring temptation to hang around the edges because of what getting involved might cost. Significantly, apart from the generous few, only passion, which can be seen as a certain kind of loving or its reverse, moves us from being bystanders and onlookers, to become instead vital participants.

The story is quite otherwise in the case of Jesus. There we see God's total involvement in the messy business of living and dying, and complete commitment to what this entails. There was no escapism. Jesus chose the very things that we instinctively shun. A man of no ordinary importance, rejected by his own people, he kept company with those on the fringe of society. Criticised by the civil and religious authorities for causing a disturbance, he was finally put to death by a doubtful alliance of enemies in power, because he so stirred up their fears that he constituted a threat to their self interest. For Jesus it was not just a question of launching himself into the goal of creating on earth God's radical justice of love. The way in which this was to be achieved and the means that were to be employed were all part of his immersion in the details and process of living in time and space.

It is of paramount importance for our understanding of a spirituality relevant to the coming millennium that we are fully aware of all the implications of an Incarnational theology. In the history of spirituality the repeated temptation to pay lip service to this fact, while avoiding its literally unpleasant consequences, remains real. To be God means to be reconciler, whole-maker, bringing all things into communion. But the very meaning of Incarnation also demands that this work of God be done in a way that is still appropriate to the suffering and sinful human condition of this world. To liberate predominantly from the outside, somehow contradicts God's original purpose in the Incarnation.

The actual process of liberation must, in a very real way, take full cognisance of the actual limitations of this world.

Jesus came, therefore, into the human situation prepared to grasp what so many human beings shirk and resent. He was prepared to enter fully into God's work of healing but in a mode that would not undermine that human condition. Labouring to the utmost of human endurance, he was yet prepared to accept unimportance and powerlessness along with frustration and the betrayal of what he stood for, in the belief that this was all part of the human process. He allowed himself to be vulnerable. More than that, he accepted fully the consequences of sin and evil present in the world and took it upon himself to work with them and through them.

While proclaiming a mission to heal and make whole, to give and forgive, and to set free the poor and the outcast who were politically weak and powerless, Jesus took upon himself their situation, lived as one of them and accepted a life-style that was theirs. He struggled to remove oppression and did not fear to speak out against injustice in any form, but he also took the consequences of doing so according to the law of his own time. Jesus let the violent opposition he aroused backfire on himself. His liberating work was essentially one of repairing and rebuilding: beginning again, with the effects of evil and sin that were there. He used limited human means that were available for a divine work. So often we are challenged by the worthwhile goals that are set before us, but we jib at the seemingly inadequate human means at our disposal, flawed as they always are from the outset. This is not what we find in Jesus. In short, he saw the work of removing the ravages of evil and the guilt of sin as one of living with and working through their consequences.

2.10   The Power of Love

Only by accepting human limitations in this way could Jesus make known to us what was to be our task in this world. To explore fully the potential for living, suffering and dying was his response to the truth of the human condition. It was this positive attitude of taking life with whatever was given, wholeheartedly, which gave Jesus that self-authenticating authority which made others look and listen to him while he was on earth. He was able to challenge men and women because he had the courage to grasp what they rejected and feared. Jesus did not say 'no' to the human condition in its frustrating details. Rather, he used evil and suffering in a creative way. He said 'yes' to life, including the consequences of evil that took life away from him in his prime, so that evil could be overcome in the only way that it can: ultimately, that is, by the power of love.

Jesus was able to commit himself to such a mission because his own ego was not the centre of his life. He was wholeheartedly and singlemindedly other-centred. Jesus loved God, his Father, passionately; and from this overriding passion came his total commitment to God's will. This meant that, because he was intimately aware of his Father's love for all creation, his life was given over to setting men and women free in a work of healing rooted in love. Jesus lived and spoke one message: the coming of God's way of love. Love was the transforming and liberating power of his life that yet became fully manifest only at the moment of his death. There and then, in the very act of dying, love enabled Jesus to let go of everything, in an ultimate movement of trust that revealed the very heart of his being as an open and empty space for God. In and through his humanity, trusting God utterly in death, Jesus made known that there was, quite literally, a sacred heart to the cosmic mystery of creation.

2.11 Beyond Death to Cosmic Birth

The death of Jesus' humanity, however, was not the end of the Incarnation process. God had made himself known

47

in the human life and death of Jesus. But in reality, this was only the beginning of God's adventure. Jesus was the pioneer of a cosmic process. God became human ultimately that humanity might become God-like. Jesus made known, in the particularity of his human nature, the God-like possibility for every human being because the wholeness of God's vision included the transfiguration of all things in the divine. Jesus' death pointed beyond itself to this truth precisely because it was seen to empower a new phase in the evolving mystery of the Incarnation. It was his return to the Father but now in the wholeness of a humanity transformed in God. This reality was interpreted in terms of resurrection: the mysterious continuation beyond death of what was of the essence of human life, experienced as a fullness of life without its limitations or frustrations.

The mystery of the Incarnation would thus seem to have reached its climax in the Resurrection with the transformation of the humanity of Jesus. In a sense it had. But it had by no means achieved its ultimate purpose, only the release of the potential for its ultimate purpose. But the release is uniquely significant. For what we really witness in the dying of Jesus are the labour pains of a new birth: the birth of a new humanity born into Christ by the power of his Spirit.

The truth that gradually emerged from the faith experience of those who accepted the Christian message was that, in some mysterious yet real way, Christ was alive, active and present among them even though he could not be seen, heard or touched in the physical manner that belonged to his human existence before death. They found that such a truth could be expressed most adequately by speaking of their own lives as shot through with this presence as a dynamic and empowering Spirit given to them. But they also knew this Spirit as their own, enabling them to live like Christ in their own lives. It seemed that Jesus's death had released the Spirit of Christ as a potential for growth into God's freedom. For all who trusted in Christ had been given the capacity to live life in all its fullness. The Spirit that radiated the divine in Jesus, in the particularity of his unique person, now seemed to be liberated and made available to penetrate and so transform all cosmic reality. With the mystery of the Resurrection of Christ, all creation seemed set for its return journey home towards the Godhead.

2.12 The Open Heart: Releasing the Spirit

Nowhere is the theological vision of this truth focussed for us with such powerful immediacy than in the Fourth Gospel, in an image that is, at once, historical reality and symbolic meaning. The evangelist bears witness to the fact that in order to be certain of his death, one of the soldiers pierced the side of the crucified Jesus and that blood and water flowed from his wounded heart (John 19:31-37). This was apparently the moment of utter powerlessness, bloody death and the failure of mission. Yet this was only what could be seen. For the evangelist, this moment of humiliation was the moment of truth because it made known the truth that God is love. According to Jesus there is no greater love than that shown by the laying down of life for one's friends. This was God's greater love: Jesus loving all human kind as his friends, even those who killed him.

Instead of unleashing yet more violence, the lance that opened the side of Jesus only enabled a greater release of God's love. With the lifeblood flowing from his pierced heart came the prophesied living and life-giving waters: the symbol of the Spirit who could only be received after Jesus had been lifted up in glory (John 7:37-39).

Because of the ambivalence of the term "lifted up", it was significant for the evangelist that the moment of the lifting up of Jesus on the cross was also the moment of his lifting up in glory, for glory implies that the presence of God is made manifest (John 8:28). The transpierced human form of Jesus dying on the cross did make known the presence of God as love, even as that love of God was given as a wholly new kind of life for those who would

49

dare to take it. The glory was in the radiance of God's love: the love that was released in the Spirit.

The image of the open heart of Christ thus provides a focus for our contemplation. It has become an effective sign for a world wounded and yet loved by God, even as symbol and reality merge in this timeless moment intersecting time and eternity. We can only respond to the prophetic word and

> "Look on the one whom they have pierced."
> (Zechariah 12:10 in John 19:37)

2.13 Contemplating the Pierced Heart

> As we look upon him whom they have pierced,
> we see the pain of love
> vulnerable to the violence of a spear's thrust,
> tearing open a wound
> whose lips speak only of love:
> the crucified one lifted up on a tree,
> for God is a lover.

> But beyond, we see the everlasting arms,
> upholding him, enfolding him
> with the tenderness of compassion,
> for the one who knows Jesus
> sees the Father in his heart:
> the wisdom of God lifted up in glory,
> for God is love.

> Yet more, from within that open heart,
> we see the flowing of this love,
> living waters gushing forth, transparent and pure,
> teeming with life yet mingled with blood-red wine,
> the fruit of a death-wound
> centred by the point of a lance:
> The Spirit of Love.

As the waters flow, fanned by the Spirit's breath,
a secret stirring of love flares up
into a living flame, creating a passion of love,
waters of fire, swirling and leaping,
in tongues outreaching, catching fire
to a world becoming radiant:
Love creating love.

2:14 At the Centre, God: the Trinity

As we contemplate the open heart of Christ, our vision is focussed upon the centre of the mandala that is the heart of our pilgrimage. There we see God at the heart of all our woundedness and at the centre of reality, as love. We need to take a long look at this truth, allowing ourselves to be penetrated by the mystery of love as we see it in God.

If God is love, we know there must be relation in God: a relating that somehow finds an analogy in what human beings so value in human relationship at its most fulfilling. This is what is implied in Christian theology's articulation of the Godhead as oneness in a Trinity of persons in which the relating is a total giving and receiving in a communion of intimate knowing. This is a relating that delights in letting go and letting be, bonded only by the total gift of reverential love.

In Jesus we relate to the uttered Word that is the complete expression of the hidden mystery of God, as it takes on the face of a person we can recognise as human. But as we respond to this most compassionate manifestation of God, we are drawn by the wound within his heart towards the mysterious depths of God. We see something of the pain in the heart of God that belongs to one who so loves. It is as if we were being called beyond the threshold of an open door to the source and ground of all being whom Jesus adores as his Father and glimpse the meaning of life and creativity in the Creator. Yet even as we are fasci-

51

nated by an awareness of the transcendence of God beyond all our knowing, this God is offered to us as our most intimate and immanent Spirit. This gift is the presence of God, making a home within our heart for a life fully open to the power and wisdom of love.

What we are offered in the heart of Jesus pierced open on the cross, therefore, are three ways of coming to know God in the intimacy of faith and hope and love. Like Julian of Norwich, we see the suffering humanity of Jesus crucified, but we are led to understand something of the Trinity of God.[4]

2.15 The Trinity: Root of our Relatedness

With such a revelation of God in the Trinity, we can see that God and creation are intimately bonded because creation is the fruit of the creative love that is God. The God who is the ground of being as manifested in Jesus, is the ground of all being. This means that God is the root and bond of all our relatedness, both to God and each other. God is the radical unity that is intimate to all things who yet transcends them in the capacity to make them truly whole and interrelated.

It was this kind of union between God and creation that Eckhart tried to express through his use of paradoxical and ebullient language.[5] For creation is the joyful and exuberant creativity of God. From the still unity of the Godhead, as from a life-giving womb, flows forth the Word who gives shape and form to all creation that wells up and overflows as the cosmic manifestation of God. But the Spirit of God, the love within all true relating, bonds creation to its God, drawing it back and reconciling it to its centre and source.

Such an image suggests that there is a mothering process alive in the Godhead: setting free for life, while remaining heart and home. It calls human beings to the task of working in this world with the rhythm of this relation of love that is the innermost dynamism of God. The purpose is that creation may truly be an interrelated network, bonded in God, while becoming ever more radiant as communion.

3.

Learning from God
How to be Human

3.1 Becoming Fully Human: Christlike

The task of working within the rhythm of God's love can be achieved only as the individual humanity of each of us is made one with our deepest self where God is the ground of our being and the root of our relatedness.

We are called to such a personal integrity that will make us truly human. But it is only through Jesus as the Christ in whom humanity is personally united to God that we can become fully alive to the deep source of our being. For it is the mission of Jesus to lead us along the journey towards this kind of wholeness. Each of us in a unique manner, is to be transformed into Christ in the likeness of Jesus who is the sign of humanity at one with its Creator God.

The paradox that yet remains the truth is that we are to learn from God how to be human: for our teacher is Jesus in whom God came not only to tell us or show us the way but in whom God lived our human life. Jesus as the Christ is himself the way. But this learning is not just a matter of imitating Jesus from the outside. The learning is about being changed from within. It is for this process that the Spirit of Christ was released. Through the power of the Spirit working within our innermost heart the true Christ-self is to emerge as the new directing centre of our human life (Ephesians 3:14-21). A wholly new dimension to the Jungian exposition of the psyche's hidden and true self is thus made available to us.[6]

3.2 Knowing with the Heart

Once we glimpse, however fleetingly, that it is the unconscious image of the true self deep within us that responds to Jesus as the archetypal God image, we grasp the truth that knowing him and knowing our true self are integrally related. Our fascination then becomes an urgent desire to know him. But with the same insight, we understand that this kind of knowing cannot be satisfied with a cerebral exercise. What is needed is a holistic and experiential kind of knowing that takes our whole being into its orbit and penetrates our innermost personal depths. Intuitive, direct and immediate, it progressively centres the person in a unitive experience. Such a knowing is authentic and sure because it is uniquely personal and can best be described as a knowing of the heart. It comes with love and when it touches God it belongs to the gift of wisdom. Its source lies within the space of the heart where God is. The sign of its coming is an intimate awareness of personal meaning that sets us free to become our true selves.

3.3 Come and See

'Come and see!' was Jesus' invitation to any would-be disciples who wanted to know more about where and how he lived (John 1:39). They were to know by the experience of actually living with him who he was and what gave meaning to his life. But he always seemed to assume that coming to know him was intimately bound up with coming to terms with themselves. He asked all who felt weighed down to bring their burdens to him so that he could relieve the overburden of oughts accumulated through legalistic attitudes, along with the anxiety and guilt that had become each person's particular oppression. In return, Jesus offered his own yoke, well fitted to the shape of each one because it belonged to a call to uniqueness.

"Come to me, all you that are weary and are carrying heavy-burdens, and I will give you rest. Take my yoke upon you, and learn from me... for I am gentle and humble in heart, and you will find rest for your souls. For my yoke is easy, and my burden light."

(Matthew 11:28-30)

The term 'yoke' is significant since it is an English translation of the Sanskrit word for 'yoga', for what Jesus taught was a true yoga involving a change of heart because he called his disciples to grow beyond where they were to where they could be.[7] They were to learn from him, as a guru-teacher whose heart was characterised by gentle integrity and patience, the loving discipline of a way of life that would give deep rest to the psyche and make them both at home and alive in God.

3.4 The Yoga of Christ

The process of formation adopted by Jesus with those who would be his disciples provides us with a very practical model that can be learnt from his heart. It begins with seeking rest for the psyche and progresses towards an ever deeper peace of soul.

Contrary to what might appear, rest is not opposed to life, but its ground. This is true physically, mentally, emotionally and spiritually. We ignore the fact to our detriment for common sense and equilibrium as much as for resilience and radiance. It is the rich soil of growth for the flowering and fruit of every form of life. It is, therefore, the place where we need to begin, especially in a society which seems to pride itself on filling up every space in which we might find time just to be. The word of advice given by a prophet to a war-torn people in the eighth-century BC is as relevant for us at the end of the twentieth century AD.

"In returning and rest you shall be saved;
In quietness and in trust shall be your strength."

(Isaiah 30:15)

Rest implies a re-turning to our deepest self where God is waiting to heal us into wholeness. As we let go of our current preoccupations, we learn from the stillness to trust the God who holds us alive in love. Far more than we imagine, we need this attitude of rest and letting be for our life to become truly our life. Instead of making life a race against time, we need to live within the ebb and flow of its tide.

Jung had learnt to appreciate the value of this teaching from the Chinese concept of the Way of the Tao, when he wrote,

"The art of letting things happen, action through non action, letting go of oneself as taught by Meister Eckhart, became for me the key opening the door to the way. We must be able to let things happen in the psyche. For us, this actually is an art of which few people know anything. Consciousness is forever interfering, helping, correcting and negating, never leaving the simple growth processes in peace."[8]

We are, then, to let go of our attempts to control life, to drop our possessiveness and clinging and to receive life in a gradually discovered awareness of our own deep relatedness to all things in God. We do this by allowing our experience to come into consciousness without erecting barriers in self-defence. Such an attitude takes us into the way of faith which grounds us in the God who becomes ever more our rest and our life.

"In this nakedness the spirit finds
its quietude and rest.
For in coveting nothing,
nothing raises it up

57

and nothing weighs it down,
because it is in the centre of its own humility.
When it covets something,
in this very desire it is wearied."[9]

3.5 Our Inner Space in Focus

To come to such an attitude of openness to God in our experience, we need to exercise ourselves in the discipline it implies. In our time-conscious society this means making time in which we can concentrate the energy of our whole person on being open to God. Simply, but deliberately, we have to take time to be.

We may begin by becoming aware of our body because its posture most readily symbolises the attitude of the whole person. It needs to be both relaxed and alert because our whole being has to move from anxiety to trust. Jesus knew just how much anxiety can bind us.

"Do not worry about your life....
Is not life more than food
and the body more than clothing?
Your heavenly Father knows
that you need all these things."

(Matthew 6:25,32)

A period of focussing on our breathing gradually slows down the pace of our lives and helps physical, emotional and mental equilibrium. Adverting to the inflow and out-flow of our breath, we can become consciously part of the rhythm of the cosmos, and gently come home to our heart centre. There should be no strain in this, only the tendency to move towards a quiet awareness of the present moment.

"Do not worry about tomorrow,
for tomorrow will bring worries of its own."

(Matthew 6:34)

For our less easily controlled mind and imagination we need to find a point of focus: one word, one image, one thing upon which our wandering gaze can rest. This does not imply intense effort, just a letting go of everything else. The point of focus is simply an anchor for our awareness, reminding us of the one thing necessary to which our heart is drawing us now. It encourages us to be relaxed and alert, focussed and waiting upon the presence of God in faith and hope and love in this present moment. The rhythm is such that we are being prepared to be wholly passive and wholly active at the same time. We are enabled to remain relaxed and alert: relaxed enough to look and alert enough to see; relaxed enough to listen and alert enough to hear; relaxed enough to relish and alert enough to discern; relaxed enough to receive and alert enough to give.

The point of focus can be as small as a delicate flower or as wide as an expanse of sea or sky. But it holds us, just as it is, with all its natural vitality, even as it becomes a sign of depths that only unfold as it holds our gaze. Jesus taught us quite simply to

"Look at the birds of the air....
Consider the lilies of the field!"

(Matthew 6:26,28)

We see a tree in all its leafy splendour. But as we gaze, its associations may flood our memory. All at once it is a tree of life or the tree of the cross. Meaning is mediated as the unconscious crosses the threshold of consciousness. Still the point of focus remains a tree, and we may be aware of nothing else, but we are aware and so present to the revelation of God in all that is. We are learning to look and to see.

There was a tree in the garden,
a tree of life for our growing
where the water was flowing.

There was a tree in the garden,
a tree of death for a moment of knowing,
a tree of life and death for our choosing.

There was a tree in the garden,
not yet for the seeing:
a tree that gave life through death,
while the water was flowing;
a tree of life for our choosing
to learn through our knowing
a new way of growing
in life that is loving,
and planting through sowing
the seeds that in dying
bear fruit in their rising
to life that is God's.

There was a tree in the garden
and a rainbow touched its leaves.

3.6 The Creative Word Creating

We can, however, miss so obvious a revelation. Limited as we are, we grow moment by moment in a circumscribed area that is the now we can cope with, in any given situation. The individuality of our person needs a place of entry into the sheer wholeness of cosmic reality: a door that opens on to the mystery that is both within and beyond. This is the reason why in the Christian tradition the initial point of focus is given to us in the word of God. The Jewish and Christian Scriptures, made available through the community of believers in the way of Christ, are seen as a sacrament of all cosmic life through which God communicates. The Bible is essentially a book about life. It revels in its earthy adventure while pointing both to its within and beyond. It is a word about the meaning of life: a disclosure of God. Through its words we are brought into contact with the thrilling turbulence of human life as it meets the torrent and flood of divine life in one magnificent series of moving personal encounters.This book is the story of people fully inculturated in the world of their times where they found God. It is not abstract philosophy or analytical psychology, yet, in the guise of their times, both are present within a whole library of literary forms, linked by an ongoing story that really is a love story: the love story between God and human beings created out of love.

True to its character as a book about life, there is no attempt to hide its dark and seamy side just because God appears in anthropomorphic apparel. Most readers would estimate that more of the Bible's pages are given over to descriptions of the shadow side of human existence than to epiphanies of the divine. It is possible to find out about every kind of human and inhuman deviance in its chapters. Bloody warfare, sexual abuse, political intrigue, vengeful violence, as well as the familiar catalogue of lust, hatred, jealousy, murder, adultery and greed, are as rampant in the Bible as in any late twentieth century television programme, reflecting the experience of its age. But even to attempt to distinguish the light from the dark in these Scriptures is somewhat of a distortion. The word of God speaks somehow through every word of Scripture, without implying by that any false or uncritical fundamentalism. The power and the glory of God are there in all the messiness and failure of human aspirations, because God's love is really steadfast and endures, regardless of what human beings do.

The word of God, therefore, provides us with access to the story of life in the world from God's point of view. This means that human beings are constantly being offered the possibility of ever greater freedom: freedom from the entanglements that enslave and make us anything less than fully human; and freedom for the growth in wisdom and love that God gives to every person. The word of God is essentially a liberation story, as yet incomplete because it awaits the response of the whole human race. It is what the Christian tradition calls salvation history that is fulfilled and interpreted by Jesus as the Word of God. This means that we can only speak of knowing the word of God when we know it interiorly through the experience of gradually being changed into the likeness of Christ. But this word of God taken to heart, in the now of present experience, does enable human beings to change, to move from where they are now to where they could be.

"The word of God is living and active, sharper than any two-edged sword, piercing until it divides soul from spirit... discerning the thoughts and intentions of the heart" (Hebrews 4:12*).

So God's word is an effective word that creates us in the image of God (Genesis 1, 2; Isaiah 55:11; John 1:1-5).

Still and always is the Word:
the Word who was with God;
the Word who was God;
the Word who was in the beginning with God.

All things were created through Him
and in Him was life:
life that was light;
the vitality of creative energy.

It was this Word that God spoke
saying, 'Let there be light',
and there was light,
light shining in the darkness.

It was this Word that God spoke
giving shape and form, a distinct identity,
to formless matter, empty and void.
For God's word is a word of power,
a word that effects what it utters,
and does not return empty and void.

It was this Word that God spoke
teeming with life, multiple and complex:
bubbling forth in fast running streams,
in surging of waves and pounding of rocks,
greening the earth with fruitbearing trees,
sheening the fruit and rustling the leaves.

Exuberant is God's creating Word,
spraying the night-sky with a moon and the stars,
letting the birds fly free in the air,
giving the beasts their food and God's care.

One word alone remains to be said;
the word that repeats the truth about God.
God saw each thing that was made
and knew it was good.

Yet from the dust, a clod that was earth,
God formed an own image, like the potter moulds clay.
With dew of the dawn, God brought us to birth
and made man and woman the pride of such play.
Into this image God made them
and gave them the light of each day.

3.7 God's Initiative: the Spirit Brooding

By taming our outer activity for a time, we find a
threshold for our openness to God: a place to begin. But it
is really the Spirit of God who takes the initiative in this
process we call prayer. For as we advert to the 'inside' of
our life we become aware of the Spirit as the power that
enables us to be and to grow in a way that seemed impossible from our experience of the human condition.

Jesus knew that, out of our own resources, we would
never overcome the fear that hampers our growth into
truth, so he countered the fear in the way he spoke to his
disciples about the gift of the Spirit.

"I still have many things to say to you,
but you cannot bear them now...
the Spirit of truth...will guide you into all the truth
...and remind you of all that I have said to you."

(John 16:12-13; 14:26)

The Spirit guides us into all truth, the truth about God and the truth about ourselves, as and when we are able to bear it. The teaching of Jesus is brought back to our minds so that we remember it, as we are ready to live it. The Spirit works within and through our own spirit by means of our temperament, reconciling the seeming opposites within us: what we are with what we could become; what we fear with what we desire; what we think with what we feel. The Spirit reminds us that we must let go and let be because we cannot control the Spirit. The Spirit's presence is felt but not grasped. It is like the breath of wind that blows where it wills, creating out of the chaos of our experience the order of a new creation where we relate in the freedom of Christ (John 3:8). So the story of creation reminds us of our ongoing re-creation where new life emerges out of stillness and waiting (Genesis 1:1-2).

The beginning is with the Spirit:
the life-giving breath of God
brooding
like a mother-bird over chaos:
formless, inert matter.
The tumultuous seething chaos of matter
could be
the Scientist's descriptive beginning
if we
could go back beyond the seething
to what can't be expressed.
But it is not.
This is an artist's imaging:
a seeing into a truth of faith.

64

It is a quiet and dark image
allowing us to ponder and wait
for the signs of life,
brooding and breathing,
learning the action of the Spirit in non-action.
While the Spirit is brooding
the world is evolving.
Wait and see!

3.8 Discovering a Place of Revelation

When we have slowed down sufficiently to be present
to the place where we are, we begin to realise that we are in
a place of revelation: a place in which we can discover
something formerly unknown to us. Both the words 'revelation' and 'discover' speak of uncovering something hith-
erto hidden, in a real sense, something of mystery. We can
prepare for this, but we cannot make it happen. It is given,
sometimes for the asking, sometimes for the waiting. But
the basic truth remains. The whole world and the story of
all its peoples is a place of revelation. We discover this by
being open to its truth. This is what we learn through
prayer that keeps us in touch with the presence of God in
all creation.

As Jesus affirmed, it is the inner space that holds the key
to the place of revelation.

"When you pray, go into your inner room
and pray to your Father in secret ...
your Father knows what you need."

(Matthew 6:6,8*)

Prayer, for Jesus, was not a question of a special place
or special words, but of sincerity, simplicity and trust:
hence the 'inner room'. It simply means being open to the
Spirit, just as we are, before the ultimate reality of God
with whom Jesus related intimately as his Father.

65

The 'inner room' is the space of the heart where we are truly who we are, with our deepest desire that remains at the core of all our desires. There, in the hush that reconciles our struggling tensions, the Spirit creates a place of revelation, bearing witness to the Christ image of God in our own heart. For the space of the heart is also God's space in the uniqueness of our person. It is so shrouded in mystery that we feel compelled to 'take off our shoes' as a sign of reverence as we come near to this sacred space. For the heart is a sacred space. We know we are there because comfort and consolation inspire us with hope and the courage to be.

3.9 Responding to the Word: Reflection

The word always holds within it a disclosure of God. It is God's initiative continually calling to each one of us: 'Come!' The word, in a sense, is a bridge between the Spirit of God and the human spirit. But this distances the relationship too much, because the word is activated by the Spirit of God who touches our spirit from within.

Revelation, however, is only fulfilled in human response. The word must be received and earthed in each person's experience. Every human being has the potential to become a unique reflection of the Word of God in human terms. But in order to become so we need to practise the art of reflection in relation to the word in the way that Jung has explained.

"Reflection should be understood not simply as an act born of human freedom in contradistinction to the compulsion of natural law. As the word testifies, 'reflection' means literally bending back. Reflection is a spiritual act that runs counter to the natural process, an act whereby we stop, call something to mind, form a picture, and take up a relation to and come to terms with, what we have seen. It should, therefore, be understood as an act of becoming conscious."[10]

The process is one of growth, taking time as the word works through the whole gamut of the human thought and feeling pattern, in imagination, intellect and will, until it comes to rest in the heart. As a discerning light in the dissenting darkness, the Spirit of truth interweaves our understanding of the word of God with our own experience until a Christ shape is formed in the unique pattern of our life. Then we become aware of the authentic word of God speaking to us in a personal way. Our knowing becomes deep and interior: a knowing of the heart. From such a centre we are aware of being energised by a spiritual power to realise and so make real, the truth of this word and to give it flesh in our lives. We sense that it is pointing towards a wholeness that makes us feel we belong to the cosmic flow of life.

3.10 Meditation: Reflecting on the Word

Early in the Christian tradition the term 'meditation' was applied to the prayerful pondering on the word of God in the way that Mary, the Mother of Jesus was said to ponder in her heart all that happened to Jesus (Luke 2:19).

The exercise of meditation begins with the reading of a short passage of Scripture. We mull it over, ruminating on its meaning until the Spirit seems to arrest our attention before one word or phrase, and we feel ourselves addressed personally. We rest in this moment for as long as we find helpful, savouring all it brings, while allowing the word to resonate in our heart.

If memories are evoked by this reflection we allow them to come, both for healing of the past and to challenge us to new beginnings as our life opens into the future. The Spirit is at work in the whole process, leading us into the truth we are able to hear in the now of the present moment. So we can trust our memory. It provides the key to making the word of God our own so that it can be personally enfleshed in our life. It holds a relevant if apparent distraction. Other distractions we can just quietly ignore.

We respond as we are able, asking God for what we want and know we need for our growth into the way of Christ. This kind of conversation is the way to an ever deepening relationship with God that is at the heart of prayer. Isaiah's servant of God could speak of the effects of such reflection on the word in what he heard and what he spoke.

"The Lord God has given me a disciple's tongue that I may know how to sustain with a word the one that is weary. Morning by morning God opens my ear and wakens me to hear like a disciple" (Isaiah 50:4*).

3.11 Meditation: Prayer of the Heart

This kind of reflective meditation can lead quite naturally into the type of meditation which involves repeating a treasured word or phrase of Scripture, often called a mantra from its use in the Eastern tradition of meditation. [11]

The word is repeated so that it is learnt by heart, not by dint of mental effort but through loving familiarity. The psychological effect of repetition has long been appreciated by many religious traditions as well as by modern advertising. The very exercise of repeating one word can still overactive thought and imagination and enable the word to penetrate ever more deeply as it descends from the mind to the heart. Again, memory holds the key to the inner process although in a different way. The repeated word, usually a name for God, like 'Jesus' or 'Abba', or a prayer to God, like 'Come Lord', simply becomes an aid to remembering the abiding presence of God. It operates not only at the conscious but also at the unconscious level of our lives and so helps to unify our inner life, integrating mind and heart, conscious and unconscious, while healing the psyche.

A further dimension can emerge when the repetition of the word is gently linked to the body's rhythm of breathing so that the unifying process extends to the whole person. Eventually the emphasis is less upon repetition than upon simply listening to the word echoing deep within the silence of our heart. This is prayer of the heart as our breathing itself becomes the prayer of the Spirit in us.

Such prayer that is both deep and simple, is learnt directly with a new kind of immediacy in times of stress and pain of heart as love breaks through the wound in our heart compelling us to cry out for what we need. It is the prayer of God's sons and daughters because God has sent the Spirit of his Son into our hearts, to cry out for us 'Abba! Father!' (Galatians 4:6). It is prayer that makes straight for the centre target like an arrow of love.

> Jesus
> the only way
> that I can hear
> the word that's spoken
> now so near.
>
> Jesus,
> the only way
> that I can see
> all that the Father
> means for me.
>
> Jesus,
> the only way
> I can begin
> to let the Spirit
> breathe within.
>
> Jesus,
> my weary head
> has found its rest
> in the beating
> of your breast.

Jesus,
this alone
can be my prayer
your pierced heart
wide open there.

3.12 Contemplation: Looking at Jesus

We remember that to anyone who wanted to know him Jesus gave the invitation: 'Come and see!' Knowing meant personal experience gained by seeing for oneself. Contemplation implies this kind of knowing. Literally, it means taking a long and penetrating look at the sacred space where God is until we really see.[12]

Once the Word of God has personally taken on the human form of Jesus, however, there is no more sacred space on earth than his presence. Jesus is the human manifestation of God, uniting in his person the spiritual potential of humanity and the hope of all creation. As our most significant point of focus, therefore, Jesus has the power to centre all our energy in a joyful release of self that is adoration. Here the passion of love finds its most authentic freedom and appropriate object because the humanity of Jesus is the perfect icon opening into the presence of God. All that can be uttered about God is expressed in the Word and that Word of God is made known in Jesus as the Christ. John of the Cross comments bluntly that we would be foolish to seek for further personal revelations instead of fixing our eyes on Christ.[13]

Jesus, however, is not only the revelation of God. He is the prototype of our response to God. Looking at him we learn how to be human. From him we learn his feelings and preferences, his desires and attitudes, his values and choices so that they may become inwardly alive in us.

It is, then, through contemplation that our lives are to be rooted in the heart of Jesus. This means meeting Jesus in all the reality of his humanity in time and place, as we find it in the Gospels, but with an openness to the mystery of God who can be encountered through him. Such a way of contemplation presupposes the presence of the glorified cosmic Christ working through the power of his Spirit in those who believe and hope in God.

Such contemplation, however, also makes use of our ability to look long at icons and the paintings of sensitive artists or to imagine the appropriate scene in the Gospels. We may begin by looking at the persons present and what they are doing, while we listen to their words, entering more and more realistically into what is happening until we see how Jesus wants to be for us, as we are led by the Spirit and are able to respond. The Gospel stories lend themselves to such visual imagination, but the purpose of the approach is to facilitate an encounter with the person of Jesus, so that we may come to know him intimately.

Jesus may become very real in such a contemplation. We should let him penetrate our gaze and hold us in his presence, waiting upon what is happening and resting in his love. We may have begun our prayer time trying to be present to Jesus in the Gospel but somehow the mystery of Christ, hidden in the story, comes to us. In Jesus God is present to us. The sense image we have looked at becomes a window through which it is given to us to see. Our response is to receive gratefully.

As the Spirit takes possession of the depths of our being, we may even be gifted with what seems like inner sight and hearing, and a certain inner sensing that relates to touch and taste. In God's gift of contemplation we are present to the presence of God, and so what we may call the spiritual senses come alive. In this kind of communion there is oneness, experienced but not analysed.

It is this seeing and feeling of the heart that brings us to an authentic interior knowing of Christ that can change our lives. Reflection in this experience is not a matter of any inner activity that we can initiate. It simply means being inwardly still and receptive to mirror the human face of

God that we have contemplated. The reflection is the gift of the Spirit in the sacred space of our heart.

3.13 Contemplation: a Reflection in the Heart

This kind of mirror reflection in the stillness of our heart reminds us that in the end contemplation is a free and gracious gift of God. But it is the way in which Jesus, who is himself the Way, wants to lead us to the truth that is life.

We may begin our contemplation by looking long at Jesus knowing that he is the living temple of God. But what God wants is that, through the Spirit of Jesus, our hearts may become in reality, what they are potentially: a sacred space for the presence of God. This means becoming progressively more transparent to God in the humanity that is given to us.

As the Spirit moves within us, contemplation gradually becomes more and more the silence that echoes the word and the stillness that reflects the presence of God. Our task is the ever more generous response of letting go and letting be. We are to allow the Spirit gently to guide us into becoming quietly receptive to whatever may be for our growth, so enabling us to reflect the radiance of Christ in our own life. This is our truth.

Growing Christlikeness is the test of the value of this kind of contemplation. It is the criterion by which we discern our need to go on persevering in its practice, however dark, empty or quiet the experience may seem to become. We may be led beyond all images and symbols, just to be present in a naked kind of faith that echoes our deepest, if unfelt, desire for God. Contemplation, then, is more like a blind stirring of love, reaching out from the still centre of our heart. But sometimes the blind stirring of love seems to come alive and we sense it as though fanned to a living flame: a gift of God for our consolation. These phrases are reminiscent of the author of The Cloud of Unknowing who teaches this kind of prayer when our inner journey takes us further into the darkness of faith. He suggests that we may have our reaching out to God wrapped up in one word that we fasten to our heart as a way of anchoring our prayer. We are to use it, like a dart of longing love, to pierce the thick cloud of unknowing and not to give up whatever happens.[14]

Still, however we experience such contemplation, it is the Spirit of God, praying deep within us (Romans 8:26). In graced moments we know by experience that this is true.

3.14 The Heart of Prayer: Adoration

We have been considering some of the ways of praying that are based upon the word of God. In practice there is much overlap in the use of the terms to describe them. But the important thing about methods is that they should only be used as they help any one individual at any given time. The best way to pray is always the way we pray best, now.

We can only begin where we are and as we are. Our truth such as it is of temperament, mood, character, age and place is our reality. We begin there, as we feel and think, and ask God for what we want. God responds to the sincerity of our truth, drawing us gently but firmly as we are able. In our response there should be no strain, no attempt to force the pace. But once we have decided to open ourselves to God, it is our task to respond with ever growing trust. So much depends upon our capacity to receive what is being given to us, just for the taking.

What remains constant throughout is the power of the Spirit of God at work in the word and the mystery of the Incarnation. We may begin either with the word of God or the Word of God Incarnate in Jesus Christ. In the end, however, the word must resonate in our hearts so that ultimately it may become enfleshed in our own lives. Prayer really takes off when the Spirit makes the word at home in our hearts and it becomes our own. Ultimately all ways of praying converge and are concentrated in the prayer of adoration: the deepest prayer of our heart where we recognise God as God, and let him be the God of our own heart. There we give ourselves to the Trinity of God living their life in us. Jesus pointed towards this fulfilment when he promised that he and his Father would come and make their home in anyone who loved him and kept his word (John 14:23).

4.

Contemplation and Discernment

4.1 Gospel Images of Contemplation

Two Gospel stories can image for us a disciple's approach to contemplation. The first simply sets the scene and our stance before contemplation (Luke 10: 38-42).

Martha of Bethany is acting as host to Jesus who is her guest. While she is busy preparing the meal, her sister Mary is sitting at the feet of Jesus like a true disciple, looking at him and listening to his words. Martha was appropriately busy, but also anxious as we all tend to be in our everyday life. But in the story, according to Jesus, Mary is doing the one thing necessary. She is learning from him the unique call of her life. Contemplation enables us to do just that. But when we have come to this inner knowing of God's way for us, it is intended that we shall be free to be busy, like Martha, about the many things God wants of us for Christ's mission in the world, only not so anxious!

The second story helps us to understand how an exercise in contemplation could operate in a particular life (John 4:4-42). If we look image by image at the Gospel story of one woman's relationship with Jesus, we could discover, through the contemplative process, something of our own story mirrored in it. It sets out, as a story, a human response to Jesus' invitation to receive the gift of his Spirit.

4.2 The Woman at the Well

Jesus was sitting down by Jacob's well in Samaria, tired and weary because of his journey, when a Samaritan woman came there to draw water. The woman was surprised when Jesus asked her for a drink because the Jews did not normally have any dealings with Samaritans, whom they saw as members of the unorthodox fringe of their religious tradition. Apart from that, this was a Samaritan woman. Jesus, however, persists in the conversation, but the words hint at a depth beyond the obvious.

> "If you knew the gift of God, and who it is, saying to you, 'Give me a drink', you would have asked him, and he would have given you living water."
>
> (John 4:10)

The woman does not understand. Jesus is speaking out of her depth. But she is beginning to be fascinated by him, and somehow she brings the question of meaning into her response which is still very much on the practical level.

> "Sir, you have no bucket and the well is deep. Where do you get that living water? Are you greater than our ancestor Jacob who gave us the well?"
>
> (John 4:11,12)

The well is deep. The source of this living water has captured her imagination, but so has the person who is speaking to her. Jesus presses home with the truth he wants to share, regardless, or so it seems, of the woman's practical questions. Yet he is carrying her with him. Jesus senses in the Samaritan woman an eagerness and an openness to something new and deep, for all her apparent lack of understanding. So he shares his secret about living water.

> "Those who drink of the water that I will give will never be thirsty. The water that I will give will become in them a spring of water welling up to eternal life."
>
> (John 4:14*)

However she understands the words, the woman wants the water that Jesus has to give and so she asks for it (John 4:15). The living water is at once the gift of Jesus and an inner spring, welling up from deep within, giving life. With this woman, Jesus had begun his mission of giving the good news. She is ready simply because she wants it. But now Jesus can move on to the next stage. The woman wants the gift, but now she must look at her capacity to receive.

4.3 Adoring God in Spirit and Truth

Jesus has shared a truth about God and his gift with the Samaritan woman, now he wants to lead her gently to look at the truth about herself and her own life. He asks the woman to call her husband. In the conversation that follows, it emerges that she has had five husbands and that the man she is now living with is not her husband. There is no attempt on the woman's part to deny or hide all that this suggested about her past. There was, instead, an incredible openness in this woman to her own truth. Jesus appreciates and warms to her honesty, not surely without a certain measure of humour, given the woman's next response in which she deftly moves the conversation to yet another level, while acknowledging Jesus' insight into her own situation.

With her response, "I see that you are a prophet", the woman owns to the fact that Jesus for her is not just any man, in the same way that she owns and accepts that Jesus knows her darker shadow self. But such honesty and simplicity make it possible for her to bring before her prophet deeper questions about the worship of God which puzzle her, and still puzzle many seekers after truth.

The symbol of the dividing line between Jews and Samaritans in Jesus' time was the fact that they each worshipped on different mountains: two different places. The woman would like Jesus to deal with this but Jesus is not concerned with taking up the question of different places in which worship should be offered. His answer goes much deeper. He is more interested in the quality of worship that develops what he has already said about the living water springing up from within, as he makes clear in his response to the woman.

"The hour is coming, and is now here,
when true adorers will adore the Father
in spirit and truth,
for the Father seeks such as these to worship him.
God is spirit, and those who worship
must adore in spirit and truth."

(John 4:23-24*)

It is not a question of places in which to worship. We can worship in places but they remain external symbols of the worship that, in its essence, takes place within the centre of our being. True adoration springs from the heart where the living water wells up in the truth of our own spirit. It is a mysterious statement and yet one that we can intuitively understand, in terms of sincerity and immediacy, as being authentic. The authenticity of our worship of God necessarily depends upon our readiness to face the truth about ourselves deep within our own spirit. Whatever her past, the Samaritan woman had demonstrated, already, this kind of sincerity of heart, so she is coming very close to letting her whole life be changed by Jesus. Two truths are meeting: the truth of God and the truth of self. According to Jesus' own words we are moving in the direction of true worship. Jesus is the Word of Truth. We are to worship God through Jesus and with Jesus in his Spirit: the Spirit that is his gift to us in the living water welling up within our own spirit. Our heart is the place of adoration. It is there that God receives our worship in spirit and in truth.

4.4 A Place of Revelation

The Samaritan woman now seems to have arrived at the threshold of adoration without realising it. What is obvious is the fact that her whole being is focussed on the person of Jesus and so Jesus sees that she is ready to know the giver of the gift. He has been leading her gently all the way to this moment. He knows that she is ready for it now because she has begun to talk about the Messiah, the Christ, the one sent by God. She remembers, and articulates her memory, that when the Messiah comes, he will make the mysteries known and answer all the questions. At this moment of her readiness, Jesus makes himself known, saying to her, "I am he, the one who is speaking to you" (John 4:26).

This is a moment of revelation. Jesus lets the woman know who he is. The woman has been waiting for this moment, only she would not have been able to say as much. We all need and want to adore. All our lives, consciously or unconsciously, we are seeking for someone to whom we can give ourselves utterly: someone whom we can love totally, and who can receive us in this way. Even in our deepest and happiest relationships we can feel this inability to let go of ourselves as we would desire. Sometimes this emerges as a problem in our relationships. We try, albeit unconsciously, to make someone else a god by making that person cope with the whole of ourselves. We demand too much from them as other human beings. For within this kind of desire is the need to adore. What we need is God. We need to pour ourselves out to God: to that ultimate loving reality that can receive us totally. Then all our other relationships have a chance of finding their own place. Finding the object of our adoration means finding that unifying focus that can give rest to our heart and make it free to truly love. At this moment of revelation, the Samaritan woman found the object of her adoration in spirit and in truth.

4.5 Freedom for Mission

The Samaritan woman's reaction to the moment of revelation is interesting for our understanding of a process of
conversion and ongoing discipleship. She begins by forget-
ting why she came to the well because she has moved to a
completely new dimension of life. She came to the well
with a water pot to fill. She now puts the water pot down,
leaves it there and rushes off back to her own Samaritan
people. She has acquired a new thirst, an overriding desire:
to share what she has received with her neighbours. Her
words are clearly good news:

"Come and see a man who told me everything I have
ever done. Can he be the Christ?"

(John 4:29*)

So the Samaritan woman's gospel is simply this. It is
not abstract. It is about Jesus as she has experienced him
in her own life. It is obvious that she cares a great deal
about this man, that he knows all about her, and that she is
happy. The Samaritans whom she is addressing also know
all about her from another point of view. But it is also
clear that it does not matter any more what people think
about her. What matters is what has just happened to her.
This Jesus, whom she has just met at the well, has changed
her whole outlook. If others know how she was before,
then they will know, even more, how she has been changed:
what in fact, Jesus has done for her; who he is. That, in
miniature, is the story of salvation in one person's life.
The gospel that she proclaims is not the story of salvation
told with the objectivity of the onlooker. It is her own
personal story of salvation that she shares with those who
know the story up to now. This is its power, and so are the
results. Because they can see what has happened to the
woman, the Samaritans come to believe in Jesus and ask
him to stay with them. But then, having met him for themselves, many more come to believe in Jesus. The woman

had become an instrument in God's hands, a Christ-like figure herself, sharing in his mission on earth so that others could say like the Samaritans,

"We know that this is truly the Saviour of the world."

(John 4:42)

Here we have a life-time process gathered together in the story of one woman. The process begins with Jesus bringing the woman to faith within the context of ordinary conversation. She in her turn follows, seemingly quite naturally, the same pattern with the Samaritans until they come to belief in Jesus. This is a spirituality that, having once found the treasure, must share and tell others all about it. Once the heart is glad, it must expand, even if it breaks in the process. It is essentially a spirituality of mission. No one comes to Jesus alone. Inevitably we bring someone with us.

4.6 A Contemplative Outlook

This aspect of mission brings us back to the context of the whole story. The disciples had left Jesus at the well in order to go and buy food. As the woman left, the disciples returned, suggesting that Jesus might like something to eat. Jesus' response was more than enigmatic. He made it clear that his food was to do the will of the one who had sent him (John 4:32,34). This was what kept Jesus going and this was the context of his encounter with the Samaritan woman. It was the will of God, his Father that every man and woman should be open to receive the gift of God and come to know and experience God, the giver. Realising all this mystery, Jesus stops for a moment. He ponders on the will of his Father and then reminds his disciples of the great harvest of humanity that awaits their sharing in his work: God's mission. What we hear is Jesus being quite lyrical. It is truly contemplation in action.

"Look around you, and see
how the fields are ripe for harvesting!"

(John 4:35)

Jesus' thirst and hunger is for the will of the Father concerning the harvest. This puts an urgency into Jesus that energises him, whatever he feels like, even tired and weary sitting beside a well. The result is that the woman now feels that she too has a new power and spirit within that enables her to live and penetrate the truth: her own and the truth of God. She is not cowed by the thought of her own weakness or sin. She has learnt and is learning to trust the way in which God works, precisely through all that is her own story when shared with faith and compassion. She knows that God loves her as she is, in her own truth, and will work through her trust, and enable the spring of water to well up and flow out into a mighty river for others until it returns home with them into the ocean of God.

"With joy you will draw water
from the wells of salvation."

(Isaiah 12:3)

The Samaritan woman had done just that.

4.7 Drawing the Living Water

There is an image suggested by this story of the living water that we might find helpful when we come to pray on a word from Scripture. It is the image of the well. The well is our own heart and our heart is very deep. In the depths of our heart is the Spirit of God. Here is the source of the living water. What we need, to draw the water, is a rope with a bucket attached. The rope is the word of God, any word on which we choose to ponder or rest. We, so to speak, drop the word into the well. This enables us to contact the Spirit of God deep within our own heart. We are bringing the water to the surface of our life. As the word takes us from the mind to the depths of the heart, we draw upon the living water of the Spirit that comes alive in us, bubbling and welling up into a new kind of life. This is the life of the Spirit, the life of Christ, the life of God. This is the beginning of eternal life, here and now, in our very ordinary circumstances, in our humanity, just as we are. This is the gift we are offered: the gift that is symbolised in the story of the Samaritan woman; living water, touching us in spirit and in truth.

> Living water,
>   water flowing,
> water flowing from Christ's side.
> Living water,
>   water of life,
> life of God that will abide.
>
> Living water,
>   giving the Spirit,
> Spirit of God aflame.
> Living water,
>   Spirit afire,
> giving life in God's name.
>
> Living water,
>   making God's home
> deep down within your heart.
> Living water,
>   calling the Father,
> sharing with you the Son's own part.
>
> Living water,
>   to know the Father,
> and Jesus Christ His Son.
> Living water,
>   Spirit of Love,
> that all of us may be made one.

4.8 Discerning the More of Greater of Love

Once we have allowed our lives to be searched by the word through our contemplation of Jesus, we come to recognise the voice of his calling. This is the beginning of an ongoing process of discernment. Having discovered God through the key of the word, we learn to discern the creative presence of God amidst the adventure of life in the world, along with our own particular place in it. Discernment is wisdom applied to our everyday life. It is alive and active in the dynamic process of being open to the Spirit through the regular rhythm of prayerful contemplation and reflection upon our experience. Through it we are guided by the Spirit along the path that lies just ahead of us, as the time becomes ripe for realistic choice and commitment.

In the Sermon on the Mount (Matthew 5,6,7) Jesus gives us a process of discernment that has been adapted throughout the Christian tradition. We find him adopting a model which offers an alternative path approach, giving his teaching for a truly human lifestyle, in contrast to a legalistic approach to life represented by the scribes and Pharisees.

Jesus' intention was not to oppose law as such but to point out the spirit of loving compassion with which it was to be applied and by which it was to be interpreted (Matthew 5:17). So he began by stating categorically,

> "Unless your righteousness exceeds
> that of the scribes and the Pharisees
> you will never enter the kingdom."

(Matthew 5:20)

Moreover, it soon became clear that the lifestyle Jesus was talking about involved something more than could be assessed in terms of keeping a law.

> "If you greet your brothers and sisters,
> what more are you doing?" (Matthew 5:47)

It was concerned with an ongoing call to ever greater love and generosity that is discerned in the uniqueness of a personal life.

Jesus, therefore, took care to expose the gulf that existed between the two standards, represented by the two ways, when he stated emphatically,

"No one can serve two masters."   (Matthew 6.24)

and advocated instead a singleness of purpose that would

"Strive first for the kingdom of God."

(Matthew 6:33)

because he understood the crippling fear contained in the desire to please those who have power over us. Jesus saw this as a subtle temptation that could only be overcome by trust in God as the one who knows not only what we need, but also our tendency to be anxious. He knew that the key to the "more" of greater love lay in the simplicity of a heart that had found its treasure in God (Matthew 6:21-23).

For Jesus, therefore, the process of discernment is about setting us free to respond to God and life in the authenticity of our real self. In a life open to the Spirit we are always being called to an ever closer union with Christ. It is in this sense that we are to understand the 'more'. It becomes what is appropriately more: the more realistic as well as the more generous thing for any one person to become more human and so more like Jesus. This is the greater love to which Jesus invites us.

There is a story in the Gospels of a rich young man who came to Jesus asking what more he could do, since he did keep the commandments of the law (Mark 10:17-22). Jesus gave him a look of affirmation, but knowing that he was capable of greater generosity, suggested something more that was appropriate to *his* growth.

"You lack one thing; go, sell what you own and give the money to the poor, and you will have treasure in heaven; then come, follow me."

(Mark 10:21)

The particularities of the story are not so important for us as the pattern of the more that is being questioned and invited. It belongs to a progression in the story of every calling.

In moments of deeper contemplation the Spirit enables us to discern within our own experience the way in which we are called to be for God: our true identity. So often there is just one thing that is wanting to us at any particular time and this is the 'more' that is being asked of us. It is our way of following Jesus now. The rich young man did want to follow Jesus but for him one thing stood in the way of actually doing so. For us, too, one thing is sufficient to show us who and where we are and what hinders our growth. This is for our discerning.

4.9 Discovering our Unique Calling

We come to know the greater love in the more that is being asked of us when our response gives us true consolation. An inward peace makes us feel that we are our true selves and we discover the courage to face the unknown of the future with trust. The confirmation of such a call may come to us in a blinding flash of insight or as an overwhelming sense of inner serenity. More often the call comes as a recurring sense of being drawn in a particular way that makes it feel right for us now. It can be tested by using our reason to weigh up the arguments for and against.

Testing is an integral part of a discernment process, for which Jesus gave a ready criterion, when he said,

"You will know them by their fruits."

(Matthew 7:20)

We are to know the origin of an apparent inspiration by assessing its orientation in the fruit it produces in our lives. Some of the fruits that should be manifested in a lifestyle inspired by Jesus are listed by Paul as love, joy, peace, patience, kindness, generosity, gentleness, faithfulness and self-control (Galatians 5:22). This is another way of saying that whatever builds up a community and makes for harmony and peace in relationships is likely to be of the Spirit of Christ.

The assumption is that genuine happiness is a sign of the Spirit's action. Conversely, confusion, paralysis, discouragement and misery are negative signs suggesting all is not well. God works through the whole gamut of our experience, so we must use it wisely, along with the counsel of those who know us.

Discerning love, however, does normally need time and on-going reflection so that we can compare our feelings in different situations, to see how they resonate with those that ring true to our deepest self. Given only one note of music, we cannot recognise a melody. We need to hear several notes before we can sing the tune: the song that God wants us to sing and we are able to sing, with courage and confidence, because it is our own.[15]

4.10 Our Desires and Our Dreams

As a practical point for progressing in discernment, it is good to keep on asking ourselves what we really want and to go on probing ever more deeply with the same question, until we begin to discern the deepest desires of our heart. These somehow meet what God wants for us because God wants us to find our happiness by becoming our true self and not a copy of anyone else, however good. God knows our potential and wants our growth for its fulfilment. Neither God nor we ourselves can really be satisfied with anything less. So we need to listen to the desires of our heart. They hold the key to our future in and for God.

Desires emerge in our conscious reflection, but our dreams can also help us to get in touch with the desires that are dormant in our unconscious. God is at work in our unconscious, and dreams are one of the ways in which we can let life come to us and become aware of undeveloped possibilities, because in our sleeping dreams our conscious self is no longer in control. Our dreams provide us with concrete picture images of different aspects of ourselves, in the men and women we meet in our dreams. There we can see our feelings, responses and reactions as they are in the raw. Such images may activate our memories and bring to consciousness past experiences which need healing, in much the same way as active imagination can put our memories on the alert. If we enter into dialogue with these images, they can become symbols of meaning for us. They can help us see where we project on to others those aspects of ourselves which we feel least acceptable, or conversely, to recognise those seemingly unattainable ideals in others, that we would like to appropriate. There is no absolute key to the interpretation of such images. So much depends upon trusting God in the flow of life and the truth of our memories and feelings. But reflecting upon the symbols our dreams open up before us, along with the experience of our conscious life, can give a wholeness to our process of discernment.[16]

Like Jacob, we may find that a ladder reaches from our earthly desires to their future fulfilment and that God is present where we least expected (Genesis 28:10-17). When, however, we have found the shape and character of our uniquely personal call, we shall have a yardstick by which we can test any further call to greater love. We shall be able to discern the more that is being asked of us because it belongs to our personal growth to greater maturity in wholeness and freedom.

4.11 Come, Follow Me!

Our attempts to live by reflecting upon our experience in the light of the word of God lead us to the point where we understand for ourselves that knowing Jesus and discovering our own personal calling are integrally related. Through contemplative discernment the Spirit guides us along the way that is both Christ's and ours. So do we realise that we come to know Jesus only insofar as we become like him and are ready, in our shape, to be Christ in our world. We understand that to be called means, eventually, to be sent: that discipleship means mission; that the invitation to "Come and see!" implies an ongoing commitment to "Come, follow me!"

It is this truth about a Christ-like life that is imaged for us with such clarity at certain moments in the Gospel story of Peter.

Peter was an impulsive, generous, hardworking and outspoken fisherman. All these characteristics, together with their positive and negative possibilities, would remain as the temperament and character of the Peter known to those who were closest to him. From the beginning of his call Jesus explored, developed, pruned and blessed the person of Peter. Always he remained Simon Peter, but step by step as Jesus called him to be disciple, friend, apostle, pastor, preacher and finally martyr, Peter became the ever more steadfast rock upon which Jesus could rely for the progress of God's mission on earth.

Significantly, Jesus preached to the crowd on the shore of Lake Galilee from the boat of Peter the fisherman, before he called him. This was after a futile night when Peter had caught nothing (Luke 5:1-11). Jesus asked Peter to launch out into the deep yet again, only to help him haul in a seemingly miraculous catch of fish. The key to Peter's personal vocation in the future was in this image of his present life.

Peter's hesitance, aware as he was of his sinfulness and weakness, made no difference to Jesus' choice of him at this moment or in the future. Jesus only calmed Peter's fears, showing him how he would still be a fisherman, only from now on his catch would be human beings. But, as a disciple sharing in the mission of Jesus' ministry, Peter would always have to remain prepared to launch out into the deep. He would need to learn to move across familiar boundaries and to take on the risk of the as yet unknown and untried. But in the call there would also be something familiar that fitted Peter's temperament, gifts and limitations. They would all be used.

Like Peter's, our call and ministry will also be peculiarly ours, while bearing within it the power of the mission of Christ at work in us. Our process of discernment will help us to discover how this can be true for us as it was for Peter.

4.12 Launching a Personal Vocation

The story is told of how one evening, after the disciples had helped Jesus feed a particularly large crowd gathered to hear his teaching, Jesus had gone into the hills alone to pray (Matthew 14:12-27). Meanwhile, the disciples had begun to cross the Lake of Galilee when a blustering storm left them struggling with the wind and the waves. The experience symbolised much of their future ministry and was clearly all part of their formation to share Jesus' mission.

Suddenly, out of the darkness, Jesus came towards them, apparently walking across the water. Seeing the phantom light, the disciples were terrified and cried out in fear. Jesus reassured them with a characteristic word, inspiring them with a new kind of courage coming from his presence.

"Take heart. It is I. Do not be afraid."

(Matthew 14:27)

There is a revelation in the word "It is I" that belongs to the name of God in the Jewish tradition but the revelation also initiates a deeper mode of discernment. 'It', whatever 'It' happens to be, either for the disciples in the fury of the storm at sea, or for us in the context of our daily lives, 'is I'.

Whatever happens to us brings with it the presence, power and comfort of God in this present moment, so we need not fear, not even the raging waters of life's darkest moments, or, being afraid, we may learn to trust. So in Peter's response to Jesus we have a model of what could be our mode of discerning God's will and presence as we attempt to sift through any situation.

> "Lord, if *it* is You, command me come to you on the water."   (Matthew 14:28)

This is Peter's way of saying that he, like us, needs to know that 'It', whatever 'It' is, is the Lord. Jesus' response provides the bridge across the present into the future to where he is calling us, as he called Peter with the one word: 'Come!' (Matthew 14:29). Like Peter, we recognise the word of invitation.

Jesus is always coming to us across the waters of life. It is for us to discern in all that happens, what is actually his particular call to us at each present moment. If God wants us along one particular path, our prayer is that Jesus may call us, saying 'Come', by the way in which circumstances open up and seem to draw us in a certain direction for our true happiness and the service of others. Then we can follow him, trusting the waters of life.

True to character, Peter steps out on to the water, confident in Jesus' call. But seeing the wind towering the waves, he takes his eyes off Jesus and, being afraid, begins to sink. Still, Peter remembers Jesus in his moment of weakness, doubt and fear, and calls out for Jesus to save him. Jesus grasped Peter's hand and drawing him out of the water, chided him for his lack of faith (Matthew 14:29-33). The whole experience was a lesson Peter would have to learn over and over again, as will every disciple who tries to walk on life's waters both discerning and trusting.

In this story about the call of Jesus and the discernment of Peter, we have seen another image of a personal vocation. The one thing necessary for each one of us is to discover our own personal vocation. It will be our way of sharing in the mission of Christ in our particular environment. There is nothing more important or more valuable for us to do; and since it is our vocation, we can do it. But we shall have to be ready to launch out into the deep. This was the theme of the song Peter learnt to sing with courage and commitment because it was his own.

"Launch out into the deep.
Cast down your net again."
"Master we've worked all night
and have not caught a thing
but at your word
I'll cast the net again."
There in the deep
it filled to breaking for them.

So great was the catch
that Peter fell on his knees.
"Depart from me Lord," he said,
"for I am a sinful man."
"Fear not," said the Lord,
"henceforth you're a fisher of men."
So they brought their boats ashore,
left all and followed him.

Launch out into the deep
where living waters flow.
God is the deep
that every heart must know.
Trust lovingly
to the Father's care.
With his Spirit filled
the Son's own life you'll share.

Launch out into the deep
life's darkest sea at night.
For Christ still needs
bearers of his light.
Go then at his word
to serve the world without fear.
In pilgrims of his love
Christ our Lord is near.

5.

A Passion of Love and Pain

5.1 The Passion of Love

The voice of such a calling as that of Christ, is towards the centre: the Trinity of God found in the heart of Christ and to be discovered within our own heart. But there is no coming to such a centre without passion: the passion of love that finds its full fruition through the passion of pain.

Passion is cosmic energy: the source of creativity and the inner force of love that attracts and drives towards union. In itself it has both destructive and creative potential. But harnessed and so integrated into the human personality, its dynamic power can facilitate the emergence of a new dimension of life and consciousness: God's gift for our wholehearted desiring.

If, therefore, passion is to be truly creative, it needs the centred light of intention: the focus of a vision worthy of its openness to transcendence, to create order in its love. This is the reason for our pilgrimage to the centre. Through it, energy has been focussed upon coming to an inner knowing of Jesus as the Christ: the one in whom we discover both God and the mystery of our own heart.

When God does become a person's centre, however, the spiritual energy released from the dynamic power of passion gains in momentum from its unified direction. Such a person is ready to be liberated from all that is not ordered to God and somehow carried in the powerful flow of passionate love towards God. Passion, then, becomes a yearning, a reaching out with every fibre of the body-person to the fulness of life and meaning in God. It is the prelude to the heart's rest in adoration and total commitment to God's mission in the world: the work of the kingdom Jesus proclaimed.

5.2 The Passion of Pain

Before the passion of love can attain to its centre target, however, it has to be purified and strengthened to an intensity of purpose that can give the courage capable of sustaining it. For this active, yearning passion of love that energises for fulness of living, needs to be explored and pruned by the passive, accepting passion of pain. This is a lesson life teaches. Love and pain do somehow work together for human growth.

The passion of love is first experienced simply as desire and longing but as we grow, we begin to know something of its rich complexity. We discover what it means to feel our hearts burst open under the tenderness of a glance. We experience the release of almost unimaginable creative energy from the passion of love and are sensitised by the joy of a consoling human relationship. Yet we also learn, mostly by trial and error, the anguish unleashed by such passion. We are chastened and humbled when we are caught up in the entangling web of a human relationship, especially when we have burdened others with the projections of our own desires. But such involvement can also lead to the counterpoint in love's music: the passivity of passion as part of the pain of love.

Nothing so expands the heart as loving and being loved, but equally, nothing can so pierce the heart, because of our sense of the inevitable inadequacy of the human response. Still, the very passivity invited by the quality of love, teaching us not only to give but also to receive, can probe depths as yet unknown. We learn to wait upon an other; and nothing so discovers our love as waiting. Waiting for a response is the lover's inevitable stance. This makes us vulnerable: capable of being hurt, as the active passion of love creates a capacity for the suffering passion of pain. From human experience it seems that the growth line of love and the discerning line of pain must intersect because the deeper penetration of love is so often experienced as a wound. Only in hindsight is its power to make whole recognised.

If, however, we have the courage to cross the threshold opened by the wounds of love, we may find that, in our very brokenness, we have fallen into that renewing centre of love: the sacred space of the heart. There we come to know the meaning of life in our own truth.

There is a meaningful Hassidic story told about some pious Jews who questioned their rabbi concerning the Shema, the passage in the Torah that is the foundation of Jewish belief:

> "Hear, O Israel: the Lord is our God, the Lord alone. You shall love the Lord your God with all your heart and with all your soul, and with all your might."
> (Deuteronomy 6:4-5)

The Jews asked their rabbi, why these words had to be put *upon* the heart rather than *into* the heart. In reply the rabbi told them that it did not belong to human power to put those words into the heart. All we could do would be to put the words *upon* our heart, so that when the heart broke, the words could just drop in.[17]

Jesus was clearly part of the Jewish tradition that understood the value of heartbreak and he has handed on the tradition.

This is the truth to which God calls us through the icon of the open heart of Christ. It is open because pierced; but opened it is a source of life.

At the level of experience there is a strange mingling of the joy and pain of love that knows of no ready explanation, so we may be prepared to believe that there is a shortcut to the space of the heart that lies through brokenness. This is the suffering that just comes to us, but especially the pain of heart that comes with the wounds of love: given and received.

If we can stay with the pain, even though the ache seems unbearable, the wound within us will open up a way into the depths of our heart. But we need to stay and pray, in the sense of just holding ourselves and the pain within the wounded heart of Christ, until we are drawn deep into the mystery of love that is God. We can only trust and learn in the waiting, until the truth has become our own because we have lived it through. Then we have learnt something of life and death but also of resurrection.

What, in short, we are being invited to see is that the real mystery of the passion of love lies in its openness to transcendence that belongs to the Resurrection. It provides the energy that can take us beyond ourselves. But this moment of transcendence is only reached when we accept to pass over from the active I'm-in-control state to the passive attitude of allowing life to happen to us and love to flow into us as a free gift of the Spirit of God. This in our ordinary human experience seems inevitably to involve some measure of pain: the pain that stretches us and so enables us to grow.

5.3 From Passion to Compassion

Clearly something new has emerged at this point in our understanding of the passion of love because of its encounter with the passion of pain. A new dimension of life has been released, enabling the Spirit of God to work more freely in the human spirit. It is the Spirit's gift of love expressed as a selfless and generous love, operating in tender compassion as the presence of God in human relationship. But we distort the truth if we see this love of compassion over against the passion of love, as though the one must replace the other. Rather is it an instance of a new kind of synthesis or synergy that is emerging.

When we truly suffer, accept the wounds at the heart of

love and so touch its centre core, the passion of love is transformed by God's compassionate love. Then we are energised by a kind of mystical passion, which sets us free for God's mission of transforming the world by love's compassion.

It was such a flame of passion that fashioned the human response of Jesus to union with the will of his Father until, in dying, he cast the flame into the earth, longing for it to catch fire. One single passion possessed Jesus at the very core of his being: its intentional focus was the Father; its dynamic energy the Spirit. For the mystery of the Trinity of God is the mystery of pure passion: passion without limits; a passion that must flow out in unconditional love; the cosmic compassion that we see as the Passion.

This was Jesus' way to the fulness of life in God: the way that he is for us; the way to the transcendence of a resurrection life.

5.4 Learning from the Passion of Jesus

What the passion process means and how we can live through it for our growth towards wholeness can be learnt from the passion of Jesus. This is true not because his sufferings are unique, although they remain a mirror in which we may see concentrated all the evil and horror of human inhumanity to all creation. But shot through the calamitous reality is the uniquely healing power of love through which Jesus transformed the powerlessness of suffering.

The uniqueness of Jesus and of following the Christ-like way lies not in suffering nor in taking away pain but in offering a way of living through it with a passion of love that changes its meaning. This was the truth Paul learnt directly from Christ so that he could say,

"I regard everything as loss because of the surpassing value of knowing Christ Jesus, my Lord. For his sake I have suffered the loss of all things... I want to know Christ and the power of his resurrection and the sharing of his sufferings, becoming like him in his death, if somehow I may attain the resurrection from the dead."

(Philippians 3:8-11)

5.5 Agony and Prayer

"Now is my soul troubled, and what should I say? 'Father, save me from this hour.' No, it is for this reason that I have come to this hour."

(John 12:27)

We cross the threshold of the Passion with prayer as Jesus did with these few words which gather up all the natural human reaction of Jesus before the imminent prospect of the most gruesome ordeal of suffering culminating in death in the prime of life. But they also indicate his awareness of this crucial moment of his path towards death as the climax of his life. Prayer, time spent alone with God, his Father, was no escape for Jesus. It was the opposite. It gave him the opportunity, which he did not shirk, of confronting, head-on, the darkness, futility and misery of the human condition. It allowed him a greater consciousness of humanity's responsibility for selfish living that ignores the injustice spawning in starvation, homelessness, cruelty and abuse that pays not even lip-service to compassion.

Nothing so heightens our conscious awareness of our human underworld as solitary and silent stillness, where our inner anguish has no outer distraction in which to hide. Its stringent atmosphere is more straining than that broad and wide space below the surface of things that is our personal unconscious. There most of us are compelled, by the force of circumstances, to meet our dark shadowy other side, as gradual healing helps us to take it back from our projections and take it off with our masks, in the process of personal growth.

Not everyone, however, can cope with the rarified atmosphere of a real dark night with its empty hollow space and resounding echoes. Without trust, too much truth can break the human frame. Jesus entered this space, and he made it holy. Jesus entered this space when he emptied himself, letting go the power of his Godliness, and taking on our humanity in its powerlessness. Jesus entered this space when he humbled himself on the ground in a sweat of blood, to hold on to an obedience of faith that would mean death. Jesus entered this space when his prayer became agony. The agony lay in knowing, with the transparent clarity of God, that his total commitment to God's mission would, humanly speaking, be a complete failure. The agony lay in experiencing, with a divine sensitivity, the poverty of his own ministry for justice and compassion, alongside humanity's failure to grasp the power of God and its inability to heal its own wounds. But Jesus did not attempt to escape.

In his ministry Jesus had done what he could to alleviate the suffering of humanity. Now he remained with the agony, and made his own final answer to the problem of suffering. He entered into it. He let it do its work in and through him. He suffered. The process, with its rhythm of shrinking from the pain, and trustful acceptance of what could not be fully understood before God, is hinted at in the Gospel story of the agony of Jesus in the Garden of Gethsemane (Mark 14:32-42).

Jesus learnt the answer to suffering by going through it in the darkness of faith. But with hope he lived his teaching: life comes, and will always come, through death. It was God's cosmic truth spoken by every seed and every tree. The earth knew it and Jesus learnt the parable for us.

> "Unless a grain of wheat falls into the earth
>   and dies,
> it remains just a single grain;
> but if it dies, it bears much fruit."

(John 12:24)

5.6 Passivity in Suffering

Giotto's painting of the betrayal of Jesus with the kiss of Judas images Jesus readiness to accept the passivity of his passion as he is handed over to all that could be done to him by those who no longer wanted him alive. Through it he gives meaning to all the passivity and suffering of our lives (Luke 22:47).

The passive mode of suffering, as response to life, allows for a self surrender inherently not possible in a predominantly active mode of being. This sounds a paradoxical and somewhat dangerous statement. It might seem to undervalue the courage of heroic action chosen freely for the good of humanity. It is not so intended. The fact remains that we can choose actively only that which is in some sense known. That which is as yet unknown to our experience, must in the nature of things always be part of the greater love that remains to be received, accepted and integrated into our lives. Suffering belongs to this category of experience.

Passivity dominates at the beginning and end of our lives but it impinges at every stage, and covers all that we do not choose and that just happens to us. The passing of time in old age makes us aware of our growing incapacity to do things and the failing of once alert faculties. Passivity comes, too, in the form of physical illness, when waiting for treatment and receiving it gives us the feeling of being simply a body, as we are called a 'patient'. Unemployment and redundancy give a new facet to the experience, with the added pain of loss of status and apparently of a useful place in the community. Most poignantly of all, passivity comes with the death of a loved one. The jagged edge of bereavement can only be suffered as we wait upon time to heal.

Meanwhile the hurts and rejection of broken relationships leave wounds which can frequently be re-opened in memory-jerking suffering at a later stage. All this, together with the deeper spiritual experiences that test our faith and hope and love to their uttermost limits, opens us to the Passion of Jesus and forces us to draw strength from his readiness simply to go through the experience of suffering in trust. For in the passivity of suffering, we are taken into a new dimension of the unknown. The pain comes from the fact that we are somehow no longer really in control of our lives. Life is happening to us. We are exposed to life and dependent upon others. We are object rather than subject, and this seems to be increasingly the truth, as life goes on. It seems that we are inevitably being directed to the quality of our being, rather than to our doing, as that which is ultimately important, without detracting from the value of our action in this world.

Such wisdom, distilled from the experience of suffering, points to hope in a future which we have yet to explore with greater attention. It is not pure chance that contemplation is the gift of God to receptive passivity. We need to allow ourselves the time and space to receive, to listen, to wait, to enjoy and to be loved, and so to discover a more holistic approach to everything that happens. A phase of life packed with various forms of activity and creativity needs a compensating phase of comparative stillness and quiet that creates a new awareness of what is, and a serenity of presence that is peace. To negative feeling about passivity, with the suffering that often accompanies it, may then be added positive feelings about the gifts and fruits it leaves in its passing. Again we are brought back to a truth that can only be learnt by experience. Suffering can only be understood by suffering. Suffering can only be suffered and what we understand about suffering depends upon how we suffer.

The approach of Christ is to do everything that can possibly be done to alleviate, to remove and to prevent suffering. But when all this has been done, we are left with the invitation to accept suffering, to enter into it freely and with a readiness to learn its mystery, a mystery that somehow holds love at its heart. This means trusting but it also means accepting with God the consequences of the gift of human freedom. Human beings are called to choose the good wisely. But they are free not to do so. The presence of evil and suffering in the world must be allowed as a possible consequence in a world of time and space. But Jesus' acceptance of suffering points to his belief in the power of God's love ultimately to use evil and suffering creatively for good.

5.7 Death or Birth: Labour Pains

Living a fully human life is a heroic and sometimes a tragic task. Few of us, however, would like to apply these adjectives to the ordinary events that make up our everyday lives. The result is that we can often miss the comedy that is also being enacted through their drama. We need to learn how to be amazed that such apparently ordinary things are used for a creative design that has long discovered the value of recycling on a cosmic scale.

Such an approach, however, while encouraging us to sharpen our perception, does not mean avoiding the obvious, if uncomfortable truth. Living a fully human life, going through what Jung has called the process of individuation in some form, does include suffering.[18]

Our egotistical self necessarily suffers from the seeming violence done to it by the emerging new and Christ-like self. It appears to lose the freedom it fancied it possessed. Loss seems more apparent than gain. But this is only half the truth. Instead, a space is being hollowed out in the core of the personality so that the Christ-self may come alive within a human heart.

We can focus on the suffering, the loss and the death, but we need not. The purpose of the process is ever greater wholeness, fulness of life, freedom and new creation: the birth of Christ in us.

It was Eckhart who popularised the bold image of the birth of Christ in the soul by constantly asking in his sermons, what does it matter that this birth of Christ is always happening if it does not happen in me?[19] Such rhetoric was meant to challenge all believers to bring the work of Jesus to completion by allowing Christ to be born in them. The image is valuable because it reminds us that the process of letting Christ live in our lives is an individual task that inevitably involves struggle and labour. We need to stay with this language of giving birth because it is, perhaps, the most authentic way of coming to grasp the meaning of suffering in our own lives as in the life of Jesus.

It was Jesus who first related the experience of his passion and death to the labour of giving birth, in an attempt to help his disciples through the difficult transition period after his death. Not only did he not want them to be trapped in the doubt and anguish of bereavement, but he wanted them to see, at least in hindsight, the whole experience as a necessary if painful way through to a totally new kind of life such as he shared with God his Father. He wanted to tell them that he understood their fear, their pain of loss, as well as their deep grief, but that this would have an end in a yet deeper and abiding joy, because his Spirit, the Christ Spirit, would return to dwell within their own hearts. To do this most effectively, Jesus chose to relate his death to the pains of a woman in labour.

"You will have pain, but your pain will turn into joy. When a woman is in labour she has pain because her hour has come; but when her child is born she no longer remembers the anguish, because of the joy of having brought a human being into the world. So you have pain now, but I will see you again and your hearts will rejoice and no one will take your joy from you."

(John 16:20-22)

Such an attitude remained within the Christian tradition that applied to Jesus the song of the suffering servant who was despised and rejected. Jesus' suffering was seen as somehow life-giving and his wounds as healing when he took upon himself the burden of others so that they might truly be born again (Isaiah 53:3-5).

Yet, even as we look upon Jesus under this image of the suffering servant, we are reminded of a truth that can apply in any human life. Strangely but truly, we know from experience that so often it is in that part of the psyche which is despised and rejected that our new, Christ-self is born. The potential for new life lies within the shadow of our personality. Pain, depression and humiliation can be the seedbed of growth. Any experience of conversion will always bring with it an awareness of our shadow. But this, in reality, is only a cause for hope. As the word of God is always discerning more truth, so also is the love of God opening up a way to new life. Healing us through our wounds and renewing our energy, Christ is being born and growing to full stature in us. We in our humanity, experience the labour pains but death does not have the last word. That belongs to resurrection as new life.

Paul had learnt this teaching of Jesus and carried over the image of giving birth to all creation.

"We know that creation
has been groaning in labour pains until now;
and not only creation, but we ourselves
who have the first fruits of the Spirit."

(Romans 8:22-23*)

But Jesus taught this secret of giving birth in the very process of dying on the cross.

Bowed and hidden his face conceals
surrendered love: in peace he kneels.

Bent and drawn in agony he hangs;
stretched and torn, love has birth pangs.

This iron and wood ask if we could
give birth to love in any other way.

105

5.8 The Shadow of Death

As we approach the centre of our pilgrimage, however, there is a crucial phase that can appropriately be called the shadow of death.

At the beginning of his farewell meal with his disciples, Jesus spoke of his death as a homegoing to God his Father (John 13:1-3). That was death for Jesus and what he wanted it to be for all who followed his way. But there remained for his humanity as for all humankind, the shadow of death. This is not the same as physical death. The shadow of death is an unknown area of darkness and anguish, imaged by our anxiety, that seems to hold us back from complete surrender to the life God wants to give us in the centre of our heart.

The shadow of death is experienced as somehow being on the harsh frontiers of existence. It stems from an acute awareness of the isolation of our separated existence as individual human beings. From different vantage points, both the mystics and existentialist philosophers have attempted to explore the deeper levels of this experience of human incompleteness. Both express the anguish it entails and see it as an ebb tide in the flow of our existence.[20]

The spontaneous reaction to such suffering that we feel powerless to curb, often moves between feelings of frustration and the temptation to despair. This can be true whether the suffering comes from unmasking the evil we encounter in the world around us or from the seeds of the same evil we see mirrored in ourselves. A kind of paralysis seems to prevent us from making any real response to life as we feel unable to give or to receive. The flow of life seems blocked so that we find ourselves spiralling into a frightening sense of our own inadequacy and powerlessness. We experience, then, as integral to our individual existence, a kind of isolating separation from God as the source of life and wholeness.

We may arrive at this hollow experience by another route or we may call it by other names, but the reality is comparable. It is what may be called the shadow of death in human experience. Jesus entered into this shadow of death as he lay on his deathbed of the cross and left us a way of going beyond reaction to response.

5.9 *From Reaction to Response*

As a beginning to this final movement in his life, Jesus prayed out of the stark reality of desolation where he was. Using a familiar Jewish psalm, he echoed the primal scream with an ultimate scream that was his cry of anguish uttering his sense of the absence of God.

> "My God, my God, why have you forsaken me?"
>
> (Psalm 22:1)

But even as his cry illustrated his teaching that we have to lose ourselves, in one sense, in order to find our true self (Mark 8:35), the trust at the end of the psalm suggests that he wanted us to remember the shepherding of God portrayed in another psalm, so that each of us would be able to say,

> "Though I walk through the valley of the shadow of death
> I fear no evil; for you are with me."
>
> (Psalm 23:4)

Crying out to God released in Jesus a capacity to respond like his prodigal Father to the unjust brutality of those who nailed him to his instrument of torture.

> "Father, forgive them;
> they do not know what they are doing."
>
> (Luke 23:34)

This was actually the truth, as it so often is, for those who inflict mindless violence. But to recognise and accept such a truth at such a moment, when we or those we love are the object of the violence, is the heroism of greater love.

5.10 Learning to Take

One of the thieves hoisted up on a cross next to Jesus gradually took in the message being lived out alongside him. In his dialogue with Jesus he demonstrated for us his well-practised capacity to take. So we too can learn how to take when we feel most bound in our pain. He simply turned to Jesus with the words "Remember me," and immediately received from Jesus the promise of a new life,

"Today you will be with me in paradise."
(Luke 23:40-43)

There was darkness all around
but I could see him:
Christ, lifted up on the cross beam.
Silent, he scarcely seemed a man,
covered with dirt and blood.
He was just one gaping wound,
a mangled form of flesh and bone,
living only to die.
There was nothing to attract in him,
yet I was drawn, like a magnet.
I looked up into his face, almost hidden
by the veil of human weakness and hate;
and I spoke.
He had given all;
I had done nothing but take.
Now, I asked him
– why, I did not know –
to give again: to forgive, to remember me.

Suddenly that face was transfigured.
My gaze was riveted on his eyes:
and I knew God, even as he knew me,
for I knew that God was love;
I had seen the living heart of God.
Then he spoke, looking at me,
and from his words I understood
that because I had believed in him,
because I had dared to take again,
he had given me God's life.
For, this day I was to be with him.
It was no longer dark.
This was eternal day, all light.
Glory streamed from the wood of the cross
and Christ made me one with him:
a good thief.

5.11 A Yearning for God

For those who sense their utter dependence for being, there gradually emerges a profound realisation of the incompleteness of human life without God. This is the beginning of a fundamental intuition of God as the innermost core of all being. Nothing is actually experienced, except the absence of being the real subject of the life that happens within us. We sense somehow that there is an ultimate reality that is both within and beyond us. It is not the individual self but it does not exist completely apart from the individual because it is the very source of all being. Faith believes in this reality as God. But now we come to realise intuitively for ourselves that human beings find their true selves not in separation but only within the wholeness of God who is the ground of our being and the root of our relatedness. So we understand why our hearts are necessarily restless until they find their rest in God.

The very awareness of incompleteness at the deeper level of our being, therefore, is also the harbinger of blessing for those who can somehow endure. The anguish that cleanses also creates a yearning for union with God as the one who gives us our identity while making us whole.

Jesus gathered up the strength of this yearning when he cried out on the cross,

"I Thirst." (John 19:28)

Obviously this was a natural cry from a body being drained of its lifeblood. But it was also a symbolic cry from the separated self of our humanity longing for union and wholeness. It was the groaning of all creation waiting for its fulfilment: the desire of love for communion. For Jesus wanted every human being to experience this yearning for their homecoming in God.

5.12 Homecoming

It is the purpose of our pilgrimage to empower us for union with God as it brings us to the space where God is at home in the centre of our heart. For it needs profound courage and a concentration of energy to go out of our ego-centred self to make space for our true self to come alive in God. This happens when love and pain meet to concentrate our heart on the one thing necessary: finding the treasure buried in the ground of our heart: the pearl of great price.

We discover our treasure when we have the courage to let God take over in our lives in a way that echoes Jesus' loving surrender to his Father when he prayed, "Into your hands I commend my spirit" (Luke 23:46).

Our response may be less serene, as it struggles with all the levels of human resistance, but the reality is there when we can ask God to take what we feel powerless to give.

Take, Lord, how can I give,
when all it means is death
and I so long to live?
Take, Lord, and dare I say, receive,
when despoiled and near despair,
but blindly I believe.
Take Lord, yes, take,
this naked nothingness I am.
Take Lord, and make
this will that will not bend.
I am yours: this utterly I know,
and you will take me in the end.
Take, and make your home in me
that being yours, I may in truth be free.

6.

A Heart for a Broken World

6.1 A Centre of Piercing Intimacy

Life can only attain to its full potential as it passes through a wound centre of some kind: a core of piercing intimacy that makes present in our lives the truth of greater love imaged in the pierced heart of Christ. For it is love and pain together that discover the sacred space of the heart.

Still, for all the labour of life's pilgrimage, coming to the centre remains the most gracious gift of God. Even the mystics hesitate to speak of such a homecoming because God, with loving courtesy, shapes its welcome to the uniqueness of each person. But with this grace, we are taken into God's own space in the centre of our heart for our comfort and consolation and to empower us for God's mission in our world.

To understand something of the ever increasing impetus towards this centre, however, it seems appropriate to listen to two sixteenth century Spanish mystics, one man and one woman whose friendship and complementarity of approach enabled them to articulate something of this contemplative movement towards union with God and the integrity of personal wholeness.

At an earlier stage in her writing, Teresa of Avila spoke of the need to seek God within. But later she wrote her allegory on penetration to the innermost mansion of an interior castle to emphasise that God dwells not simply within but at the very centre of our being.[21] Teresa chose to do this because she had grasped from John of the Cross the philosophical, theological and psychological implications of the presence of the Trinity of God in the innermost centre of our being.[22]

The genius of the insight of John of the Cross lay in his intuitive appreciation of the intimate relationship that exists between knowledge of our inmost self and knowledge of God. For John of the Cross the centre of the soul is God, so when the soul knows and loves God to the utmost capacity of its being, it will have attained its deepest centre in God. The more love it has, the more deeply it is centred in God. So in a moment of piercing intimacy, knowing the true self and knowing the indwelling presence of the Trinity of God, mysteriously coalesce. Such a grace is the effect of the Holy Spirit: the living flame of love who tenderly wounds the soul in its deepest centre.[23]

Teresa knew that to reach the state of union with God we must come to that centre within where God holds us in being. But she is equally clear that this is a free gift of God because we cannot enter by any efforts of our own. God must put us right into the centre of our being. But when this has happened Teresa indicates that we shall know in some self-authenticating way.[24]

Like John of the Cross, however, Teresa is aware that there are depths of presence to that centre where God is and that we are always being called to grow into the full stature of our union with God in Christ until death takes us into the fullness of that life. But she leaves a reflection on her own experience of the Trinity at home in the innermost mansion of her *Interior Castle* as a word of encouragement for all who make the journey inwards. For when the scales were removed from her inner eyes she saw something of the presence of the Trinity in that sacred space of the heart deep within her. In the true tradition of the mystics, it left her with an abiding memory of that interior dwelling place as spacious: large enough for us to find peace and an ever renewing source of life and love.[25] But perhaps no mystic so captures this sense of rest and homecoming to the intimacy of our inner space as the anonymous fourteenth century author who closes his fragment on the way of our desiring with such words:

> "Before the soul is rapt into God, he seeks in the first fire of love for the One his heart desires and when in this way he has sought and found his Love, he runs with a meek and ardent desire to be at home with him. And yet he does not go at once, but moves to and fro with a most ardent love, and stands piteously by with his desire of God, so as to enter into his heart. Then God, his countenance full of love, takes the soul and sets him in the midst of his heart. Then all the world cannot express the joy that the soul feels in his Lord and Love."[26]

So the constant tendency of our journey remains that of seeking within our own heart what has been made known to us in the pierced heart of Christ: the God who remains present to our faith and hope and love, even when we only sense the hollow pain of absence. For that, in itself, is a sign that we do already know God in some mysterious yet authentic way.

> Seek within
>   depths within depths
>   of love folded in pain
> Seek within
>   depths within depths
>   of silence that echoes his name
> Seek within
>   depths within depths
>   of a spear-riven side
> But still
>   seek within
>   for there is life
> Be still
>   seek within
>   and abide.

6.2 The Thoughts of His Heart

It is, however, only through reflection that we are able to grasp how death and life, suffering and joy, not only follow each other and so belong together, but can be present in some strange way in the same experience as two sides of one coin. It was through such reflection that the disciples' experience of Jesus' death and resurrection was able to be expressed in the Gospel account of the farewell discourse of Jesus. It comes to us like the thoughts of his heart to renew our faith in life through death and joy in pain and prepares for a new self-transcending dimension of life that belongs to the Resurrection (John 13-19). We may pause to ponder the meaning of the story.

> Now at length his hour had come,
> soon the Master would have to go,
> but they feared in dread and anguish
> and would not yet accept it so.
>
> They could not think of life without him,
> gone his presence from their side,
> for they had learnt to love and trust him,
> serve him as their Lord and guide.
>
> Then he spoke, their Lord and Master,
> unveiled to them the mystery
> of eternal Love's encounter:
> life within the Trinity.
>
> First he told them of the Father
> and the Spirit both did share
> by their drawing to each other
> in a love-filled gazing prayer.
>
> Then he said that he must leave them,
> go back to the Father's side,

but lifted up he still would draw them:
in his love they would abide.

Though they joyed in Christ's returning
to their God, his Father dear,
yet their sorrow at his parting
filled their hearts with pain and fear.

This the time of Christ's own choosing
to tell them why he must depart:
in his going was his coming
to dwell within each human heart.

Yes, he told them, if they loved him
did with him the Father's will,
they would know again his presence,
of his Spirit drink their fill.

Words of life in truth he gave them,
he would not leave them all alone:
with the Father he would love them,
make in them his living home.

But would they grasp this joy past telling?
Would they take this inward grace?
Would they know their God indwelling
before they saw him face to face?

Would they know the heart of glory:
love shared in mutuality;
the Father and the Son's own story,
eternal life lived inwardly?

Would they each within the other,
know the presence of their God;
and by their love for one another,
show him on the paths they trod?

So the lance in death's surrender
disclosed the glory all should know:
from his open side the Spirit
came within the water's flow.

Thus the prayer of love's submission
gave us life and made us one:
serenely turned towards the Father,
true heart's worship had begun.

6.3 Leaves Falling, Christ Rising

In reality what we call the Passion and the Resurrection are not two separate consecutive events but two complementary aspects of the same reality. The Resurrection grows within and out of the Passion, in the Christ story and as it will be reflected in ours. But for us, there is a real sense in which time is necessary for movement from one to the other. We need time for healing and to create a capacity for future joy.

No one images more clearly this time of waiting through death into resurrection than Mary, the Mother of Jesus (John 19:25-27). Through her acceptance of the suffering and death of Jesus, Mary shared in his labour of bringing forth a new creation. This she demonstrated in two passive modes of action that signified her total presence to what was happening. Mary stood at the foot of the cross. She remained steadfast in the courage of enduring faith and patient suffering before all that was done to her son. Then she received, not merely the dead body of her son, human anguish enough, as the great artist of the pieta has captured for us but she received also, in place of her son, a disciple of Jesus, and in receiving him, became the mother of a new people of God. There Mary shared actively in building up the new body of Christ. She lives now to help bring Christ to birth in others, by seeing in them, as does God the Father, none other than her well-beloved son.

117

In this waiting, Mary is the woman of faith who shows us that passion is not a quantity of emotion but a quality of commitment. Such commitment implies that we are in some measure at least, centred in our heart and so able to live creatively out of the courage that moves us into the future, not without fear but in spite of fear.

At the same time, Mary teaches us how to live through our times of bereavement: to let loss create a space that will form us for a new commitment, as courage integrates the pain of the past into a capacity for future joy. It is the lesson that Mary, as a mother, learnt from creation in the cycle of its seasons as she also learnt it from her child: the Christ of God.

> The leaves fall
> and I wonder
> at the passing of so much fullness.
> The leaves fall
> and there is silence in the air
> heavy with the mists of fruit long borne.
> The leaves fall
> and the waters bear their weight
> not just their reflection overhung.
> The leaves fall
> and life stands still
> and I wonder that it's been at all.
>
> I wonder at the richness
> of those sun-filled days.
> I wonder at the fragrance
> the roses seemed to bring.
> I wonder at the freedom
> of birds upon the wing.
> I wonder at the joy
> that made me want to sing.
> I wonder at the peace
> that's wrought in suffering –
> for I wonder at the love
> deep down in everything.

The leaves fall
and there's a dying in each day.
The leaves fall
and there's nothing I can say.
The leaves fall
and all earth's beauty falls
asleep
and I – I want to weep.
The leaves fall
and I doubt
that such beauty can ever be
again.

Yet I believe it will.
For I have known love
in a broken human heart
and seen Christ's cosmic beauty
rising from that heart.

6.4 The Body as Icon of the Spirit

The risen Christ comes suddenly. He appears in disguise: a God of surprise to human waiting. He comes as life through death, joy out of pain and peace after struggle. Out of the depths of the heart suddenly he is found: the buried treasure that we have been seeking.

In the story of Jesus' first appearance to his disciples gathered together in an upper room, we are told significantly that the doors were closed (John 20:19-20). For the disciples were closed in not only by shut doors but by the fear that bound them.

Suddenly Jesus was present to them with a word and an image for their consolation. The word of Jesus was simply an all-pervading message of peace: the surest sign of God's consoling presence. Not surprisingly the disciples were glad. But with the word came the image of his body radiant but still bearing the marks of the wounds he suffered.

The disciples might have expected that the figure of their risen Lord would not manifest wounds: an apparent scar on the wholeness of humanity; but they were to learn otherwise. The marks of the wounds came as a sign of assurance that wounds, however they are received, are for our healing and growth, and ultimately for our glory. In Jesus they were a cherished memory of love's pain. For all humanity they are an encouragement and a reminder that wounds belong to our wholeness as signs of struggle and courage in commitment.

The image of a radiant yet wounded body, appearing as a sign of God's presence in the risen Christ, however, said even more to those with eyes of faith. The risen Jesus was demonstrating yet again at this unique moment of eternity intersecting time, the significance of the body. God's ultimate purpose in the Incarnation was that the whole of creation should be shot through with the radiance of the Spirit of God. From Jesus' birth, his body had become the place where the invisible Spirit of God could be discerned. This was to prepare us for what such a truth could mean for our own existence: that the body with all its capacity for pleasure and pain, could manifest and give access to the Spirit of God. The disciples seem to have grasped this truth as they applied to Jesus' own awareness of his vocation the words of a psalm.

"A body you have prepared for me."

(Hebrews 10:5)

It is a word that we have to make our own if we follow his way into a risen life.

A body you have prepared for me
for labour, a taste of weariness,
the husk of creativity,
offsetting all my restlessness.

A body you have prepared for me
for pain, a feel of helplessness,
stretching all my limbs
to patience and gentleness.

A body you have prepared for me
for love a touch of tenderness,
healing wounds of life
with fragrant oil of kindliness.

A body you have prepared for me
for joy, a sense of blessedness,
coursing through my veins,
contentment and happiness.

A body you have prepared for me
for the Spirit you have set in me
that all my might be for you
in liberty.

6.5 Sent Like Jesus to Forgive

The experience of consoling presence, however, is never
the closure point of an appearing of the risen Jesus, only its
initiation. Beyond lies the mission: the mission of the
Father, the Son and the Holy Spirit given by Jesus to those
who would follow him closely enough to carry on his
ministry within the world of their own time. In the Gospel
story this is a moment of future orientation when Jesus
earths for the whole world all that happened at his death on
the cross. The word of peace becomes a word of mission,
and the image of breathing becomes an act of empowerment for his disciples because the Gospel word for breath
also means spirit.[27]

"Jesus said to them, 'Peace be with you. As the Father
has sent me, even so I send you.' When he had said this,

he breathed on them and said, `Receive the Holy Spirit. Whose sins you forgive, they are forgiven; Those you retain, they are retained.'"

(John 20:21-23*)

As Jesus was sent by the Father, so does he mission his disciples, giving them the power of his own Spirit as new life. What, however, is especially significant is the way in which this missioning with the Holy Spirit is gathered up into a ministry of forgiveness. The Holy Spirit is linked to the absolute human need for forgiveness. At the level of person, life is only truly life-giving if it enables knowing and loving and relating. Still, it is inevitable that we shall hurt and be hurt in our relationships, so that communication is blocked. Life then becomes frustrated and closed in. Only forgiveness, given and accepted, can enable life to flow again. As we can cramp each others lives by retaining forgiveness, so can we liberate every time we forgive. Forgiving is the life-blood of our relating, allowing God's love to be rooted among human beings. Forgiving goes before the giving, preparing the way with a generosity that is truly the life-breath of the Holy Spirit of love. So does Jesus set his seal upon forgiveness as the everyday flow of God's re-creating power in our relationships.

6.6 Touch the Wound and Discover the Heart

Thomas represents the sceptic among believers and even more the sceptic within the believer, but we have reason to be grateful for his reaction. When the other disciples told him that they had seen the risen Jesus, Thomas' need for proof apparently knew no bounds, as his words make clear in the story (John 20:24-29).

"Unless I see the mark of the nails in his hands
and put my finger in the mark of the nails,
and my hand in his side, I will not believe."

(John 20:25)

Jesus, however, knew his disciple, and understanding his needs, responded to where Thomas was at that moment. There is what seems to be a replay of the earlier appearance, just for Thomas' benefit, with all the additions stipulated by him, as Jesus invites his response.

> "Put your finger here, and see my hands.
> Reach out your hand, and put it in my side.
> Do not doubt but believe.
>
> (John 20:27)

The story is climactic. The risen Christ was asking Thomas for a response of faith, as he continues to ask it from each one of us. But he was realistically aware of the need for formation into faith. The mind, the body and the heart, all have their place in a holistic education that is the only appropriate preparation for faith.

God, above all, respects what and who we are. We see more acutely and understand and empathise better when our feelings are involved. We need to touch and taste before we judge and choose; and all these human modes of response need to be explored before we can transcend ourselves, and truly trust in the way of faith.

Christ was aware of Thomas' need for a personal experience, as he knows our need and desire for the same thing. For it is in the very uniqueness and intensity of a personal encounter that we become capable of a response of faith and trust. Reason itself works best after an authentic form of ecstasy that takes us beyond ourselves. In this context, the passion of love moves us towards a new discerning of meaning. For the heart is not only the hub of all the senses, it is also the place where sense and spirit meet, interpenetrate and are made one: the space that opens into the presence of God.

When our vision is so enhanced and our being centred, faith can really take off and help us root our vision in a practical and personal way. All this is somehow held within Christ's invitation to Thomas to touch the wounds. Touching the wound in the side of Jesus was Thomas' way of discovering the heart of Christ again. It spoke more powerfully than any words about God's love. Here was the image of tenderness and warmth, of energy and consolation that could give courage and confidence.

The visible wound was the sign of the invisible love that was its meaning. But the image is also a continuing reminder of the ever present wounds in every human being that call out for our compassion and care. We are asked to touch these wounds, to care for them and bring healing, but above all, to meet with tenderness and comfort those who bear them.

The wounded, physically, psychologically and spiritually are the poor we have always with us, as well as within us. It is not enough that we look upon those who are pierced. We have to touch their wounds by coming into contact with them and getting involved in some way with their situation. In touching them, however this may happen, we discover the heart of Christ again, and very close to us. Then we shall understand that the last appeal of the risen Christ to Thomas is also made to us, and be able to respond.

6.7 Believe and Adore: Immediacy

Before Jesus' appeal, 'Do not doubt but believe', Thomas was clearly at a loss for words. But Jesus' love and understanding drew Thomas out of himself in a leap of faith that became profound adoration. Somehow he was drawn beyond the open wound in the side of Jesus so that he knew the heart of Christ as an immediate personal experience. Then all doubt dropped away, as it seemed irrelevant. The experience was self-authenticating, so he could only give himself utterly in a faith that was adoration.

The heart of Christ had become for Thomas, what it can be for all of us: a tangible and visible focus pointing to that sacred space of our heart where God is, for every human being. So the last words of Jesus take Thomas beyond images into a new-found trust, in a life lived from that inner centre, which is where they take us.

> "Blessed are those who have not seen
> and yet have come to believe."

(John 20:29)

> I am therefore I love
> that total sensibility
> that looks at me
> out of your undefended face
> immediately.
> I love therefore I am.
>
> I am therefore I love
> the utter vulnerability
> that touches me
> from within your wounded side
> so tenderly.
> I love therefore I am.
>
> I am therefore I love
> the Godly Trinity
> that breaks through to me
> in the beating of your heart
> creatively.
> I love therefore I am.[28]

This haunting late fifteenth century painting by Bramantino, the Milanese Bartolomeo Suardi, depicts the Risen Christ showing the mark of the wound in his side. Christ stands before us, one hand outstretched. His expression suggests an appeal for faith, as Thomas realises when he hears the words, 'Do not doubt but believe.'

A Vision of Cosmic Radiance

7.1 A Vision of the World from its Heart

> "I am about to do a new thing;
> now it springs forth.
> Do you not perceive it?"

(Isaiah 43:19)

Becoming a person is different from being an individual. Individuality means external separateness. Becoming a person implies interior deepening of consciousness that leads not only to inner concentration but also to radiating expansion. The integrated person is not only centred but at the same time radiates and finds fulfilment through relationships and union with others.

Our pilgrimage has brought us to the heart: the centre of the mandala. This means that we can now look out from that centre to its radiance in the world with a new way of seeing learnt from the heart of Christ.

The reality of the world is what we hold in common with everyone in it. It is a fact, regardless of what we believe about it. This is our point of meeting. Differences arise from our vision of the world. For in being given a vision of God we are, in the same gift, given a vision of the world: the vision of a world wounded and yet loved by God.

The vision of the world that comes to us from the heart of Christ shares with others a sense of responsibility to explore and nurture the universe, but its faith values add another dimension both to the seeing and the responsibility. It accepts the inherent value of matter and humanity's role as the spearhead of an evolutionary process, but it also sees a purpose both within and beyond the evolving universe. It lays the world open to the possibility of penetration by the Spirit that faith sees at work within the process. It accepts the world of here and now but it does not stop at the visible and tangible. It sees all reality in the splendour of its being but also in the wonder of its becoming, even when confronted by destruction and evil. It looks at, but it also looks through, and sees within the world a presence that holds it in being.

With such a vision of the world, we cannot but hear the ongoing call to break through the familiar outer shell of the world we see, to discover yet more of the mystery at its heart. But the dynamic of this vision is towards cosmic wholeness through effective involvement in the world. It grasps, therefore, the place of discrimination and distinction as tools in the development of understanding and the acquisition of knowledge. But it also has a feeling for shading and the reconciliation of opposites that inevitably belongs to gradual growth and concern for interconnecting and interrelating. In this lies the vision's intuition for wholeness that gives it a unique task in facilitating the networking that enables true communion in a universe shot through with the radiance of God.

7.2 The Cosmic Dimension

The signs of the times, however, tell us that the way is being prepared for the contribution of a spiritual vision that takes seriously the cosmic dimension of life. Only a global spirituality can have relevance for the kind of cosmic consciousness that is emerging at the end of the second millennium. Anything less would be unreal. For awareness of the cosmos and unified theories of nature is becoming normal, as more and more scientists make popularly available the fruit of their research as highly relevant for ordinary life in an ever evolving universe. With the third millennium we are moving into cosmic space.

Probing questions concerning the existence of the world

are not new, but at this moment important discoveries are dramatically altering scientists' perspective on the nature of the universe. They are discovering, not only new laws of nature, but ways of thinking about nature that depart radically from traditional science. This is especially significant since revolutions in science are not just rapid advances in technical details, but transformations of the concepts upon which science is based. For it is precisely these transformations of concepts that touch the language of spirituality and mysticism. Teilhard de Chardin's mystical-scientific vision of convergent evolution does not stand alone among scientific theories concerning the unity at the heart of nature and the experience of unified consciousness. Biologists as well as physicists and astronomers are being confronted with increasingly complex structures and patterns within the cosmos, which seem to converge into some form of what we might rightly call 'concentration', the fruit of a deep 'gravitational attraction.'[29]

7.3 Science and the Spiritual

Classical physicists saw the universe as a marvellous collection of separate entities and events isolated by definite boundaries of space and time, and for which they formulated scientific laws. But the account of the twentieth century revolution in science as given by physicists themselves, demonstrates the awesome character of the intellectual upheaval that has occurred since the conception of Einstein's theory of relativity. This account makes old opposites indistinguishable, and time and space so mutually interdependent, that they form an interwoven continuum and a single unified pattern. It is said that any physicist will tell you that all objects in the cosmos are simply various forms of a single energy. Allowing for the simplifications of popularisation, it would seem that the inner unity of opposites is hardly an idea confined to the mystics, whether of East or West. In fact, modern physics proclaims that reality can only be considered as a 'union of opposites': a phrase used by the mystic Nicholas of Cusa, and much valued by Carl Jung, to refer to ultimate reality![30] As a consequence, what scientists thought were totally separate and irreconcilable opposites, turn out to be complementary aspects of the one and the same reality. Quantum theory has virtually abolished the notion of fundamentally separate objects and has come to see the universe as an interconnected web of relations whose parts are only defined through their connections to the whole. Reality is a network of inseparable patterns: a seamless coat of no boundary.[31]

It would seem, therefore, that a new vision of reality is penetrating the scientific world: a paradigm of a creative and self-organising universe in which the collective, cooperative and interconnected aspects of nature are emphasised. Its perspective is synthetic and holistic rather than analytic and reductionist, recognising that physical systems can display innovative and unforeseen modes of behaviour that are not captured by the still valued Newtonian or thermo-dynamic approaches. Such a physicist's view echoes the truth held in the non-dualism of Advaita Hinduism, or the Mahayana Buddhist view of the universe as being like a net of jewels in which the reflections of all are contained in each. The same kind of mystical language occurs when we learn that the whole universe is originally implicated or folded up together, and that what we observe, in the everyday world, is the explicate order, that which has been unfolded.[32] We cannot but hear in such an evocative if not explanatory vision of wholeness an echo of that fourteenth century mystical theologian, Eckhart, referring to the 'ebullitio' or unfolding of creation from the Godhead, and the reconciling and return of all things to their original unity.[33] All possible interconnections are latent and coordinated within the integrated original and ultimate whole.

Such language, reflecting a new cosmic vision of wholeness, finds a meaningful centre both for reconciliation and radiance in the symbol of the heart.

130

7.4 Ecological Vision and Networking

Scientific theories concerning the interconnectedness and unification process alive in nature, do not stand alone. Qualitative change applied to the universe is becoming a practical human concern with a rapidity imposed by the demanding necessity to preserve the planet we know. Environmental sense of responsibility is growing, as ecologists give us the good news and the bad news about the way we care for our world. Convergence is also apparent in real social concern for communication, as we increasingly involve ourselves in networking and interrelating, as well as in attempting to ignore space distances by making travel lines all round our globe in water, land and air, not to mention the outreach into space.

At the present stage of evolution the human species has covered practically the entire globe leaving little room for expansion. The sheer numbers of humanity, and inevitably greater physical contact between peoples, together with constant pressure on the total resources of the earth, produces an almost irresistible movement of humanity towards a collective awareness of intrinsic belonging together. Globalisation is a reality that a spirituality for 2000 AD. cannot ignore.

So far, attempts by political and economic systems to deal with the questions raised and to promote an energetic socialisation, have proved insufficient because they still operate more through external coercion than free inner choice. Co-reflection and consciousness-raising is active among groups of the poor and oppressed in search of liberation. But this only points to the truth that greater social integration will not come about by itself. Certain it is that the growing refugee problem puts the focus on the issue in an alarming way. The strenuous effort of all human beings is needed to build the earth into a true world community. But only hope can stimulate human thought and provide the necessary energy for action.

7.5 Hope: Religion Pointing the Finger

It is this star of hope which moves our gaze towards the movements of religion on our planet since the beginning of its history. Religion is about finding meaning in the whole of creation, even though so much of our practical experience of organised, particular religions suggests sectarian splintering and divisive beliefs. The basic task of religion is to point the finger to the beyond that illuminates the here and now. But, because it is a human response to a revelation of God, it inevitably shares in the limitations of the human world. Geographical situation, historical perspective and cultural expression, all colour the language of liturgy, belief systems and behavioural patterns. But central to all the major religions is the awareness of a deep inner if mysterious experience, and the attempt to interpret it, in order to give meaning to human life and the world.

In the present age it is the growing realisation of this fact that points to ecumenism as integral to cosmic consciousness. Ecumenism clearly implies some kind of synthesis, but this must not be confused with syncretism. We should not see this unity in terms of a lowest common denominator in creed, code and cult. Unity is not the same as uniformity. It does not, for example, mean that the uniqueness of Christ in history must be blurred. Rather, it means really taking seriously the hidden potential for reconciliation and universality that lies within Christianity, as it is also present potentially in its matrix: the Jewish religion of the Old Testament and in the ideal vision of the major world religions. This demands a constant effort to penetrate the truth hidden and expressed in the variety of religious forms that demonstrate differences in cultural manifestation. It means real empathy and a belief in the complementarity of Eastern and Western, as well as Northern and Southern, approaches to articulating religious experience and revelation. It means, moreover, an honest attempt to re-root and earth belief in a new transcultural future language that is not only conceptual and verbal but touched, tasted and danced with living symbols.

7.6   Release in the Heart Symbol

We must, however, go beyond the visible manifestations of religion to see its essential relevance to the process of cosmic unification. Union belongs to the inmost core of religious experience that happens in the secret of the human heart. The mystics know something of this union, and point towards it consistently as the truth of a future that is always coming, even while recognising the role of variety in the forms of worship in different cultures. Significantly, the space and symbol of the heart provides the most fruitful point of dialogue between different world religions and enlightened humanism. The terms used may differ in the Indian tradition as it develops in Hinduism and Buddhism, and in the Far East in Zen and the secret of the Tao of the Chinese wisdom tradition as well as among the Sufis of Islam. But the 'cave of the heart' remains the convergent point of unity in the hidden depths of religious experience. The teaching is, in one sense, incredibly easy to state! All human beings must seek for their own innermost centre, and in so doing find God or that which is ultimately beyond all explanation, at the heart of the human and so at the still centre of the world. Cosmic unification must have a converging centre of meaning. It is towards this that religious ecumenism points in its global manifestations. We seem, therefore, to be finding, yet again, a realistic place for a spirituality that is centred in the heart.

At this point it seems appropriate to refer to that real pioneer and prophet of a spirituality with a cosmic dimension: the scientist and Christian mystic, Teilhard de Chardin, whose vision of reality has inevitably coloured so much of what has been introduced so far. He was not attracted by the expression of devotion to the Sacred Heart, in its use of a heart symbol depicted with anatomical realism. This, however, did not prevent him from finding in the symbol of the Sacred Heart a meaning that took him beyond any representation of the humanity of Jesus, in its capacity to provide an ultimate focus for his ideas about convergent evolution of the cosmos. His own words are the most eloquent.

"The moment I saw a mysterious patch of crimson and gold delineated in the very centre of the Saviour's breast, I found what I was looking for – a way of finally escaping from everything that so distressed me in the complicated, fragile and individual organisation of the body of Jesus. It was an astounding release! As an effect of convergence and concentration, the whole physical and spiritual reality of Christ was visibly condensed for me into a well-defined, compact object from which all accidental and restrictive particularity disappeared. There was no longer a patch of crimson in the centre of Jesus, but a glowing core of fire, whose splendour embraced every contour. Through and under the symbol of the Sacred Heart, the divine had already taken on for me the energy of fire: by that I mean that it had become able to insinuate itself everywhere. Inasmuch as it was capable of being universalised, it could in future force its way into and so give a radiance of love to the cosmic milieu in which I was engaged in making my home."[34]

What seems especially significant and needing emphasis, at this point is the way in which Teilhard de Chardin focussed upon the word 'release'. While being inserted within matter, the symbol of the heart enabled him to go beyond the purely human, both to the cosmic and the divine, and so to reach a new synthesis concerning the nature of reality: at once human, cosmic and divine. He expressed this more succinctly in his journal on the feast of the Sacred Heart itself. There he said that a great secret and a great mystery is discovered in the fact that there is a heart of the world and that this heart is the heart of Christ. What may be known through reflection coincides with what is given to us in revelation.[35]

7.7 *The Risen Christ: Cosmic Radiance*

As we come to consider life lived from this centre vision, however, we need to look at the Gospel stories focussed on the Resurrection. These are not just stories of the risen Jesus remembered by his disciples. They bear within them a word of truth about the mode of God's appearing in a human life open to the Spirit of Christ and an invitation to the kind of faith that is concerned with changing the world.

A work of art, these narratives are creative in the telling, with a psychology that has an authentic ring about it as each character takes the stage for an encounter with the risen Christ. In each narrative we find emphasised certain aspects of what has already been learnt from Jesus about God's way of being human; only now the thrust moves beyond calling, to mission: the mission discovered in the heart of Christ. As we experience the story, it is intended that we too will be formed for living from the centre with a vision of cosmic radiance inspired by faith, hope and love.

Having found this centre vision, Hildegard of Bingen could say that there is nothing in creation that does not have some radiance.[36] For the call of Christ is that we should first look towards God and then be radiant (Psalm 34:5).

7.8 *Resurrection: Re-Creation in a Cosmic Garden*

In the biblical story creation really began in a garden, so it is not surprising to find the re-creation story of the resurrection taking off in a garden. It brings with it a profound ecological and psychological message that is for our healing and the healing of the nations. For it need not be trite to refer to a poetic comment about God being nearest to us in a garden. It could be true.

There is no more powerful visual image of the presence of God than a beautifully cultivated garden. Variety in form and colour, and vistas opening up new horizons suggest a God-like creativity. But the human dimension is clearly present as well. Such a garden reveals close attention to detail, sheer hard work and tender, loving care on the part of human beings cooperating with all that nature provides. It is equally true, however, that a wild landscape in a fertile valley untouched by human hand, can reveal God in its free-ranging growth. Here, where the ecological balance has not been disturbed, the phrase "untouched by human hand" implies a blessing. But from one end of the spectrum to the other, there are parables of nature for humanity where we may find God in a garden.

Creation itself is the most amazing cause of re-creation. It is a gentle healer, natural and far more effective, in so many cases, than some of our manufactured and supposedly speedy cures. It co-operates with time, waiting patiently for the particular touch of each of the seasons; but it can sometimes be an instant healer. We are near to God when we are near to the earth because we are grounded and are, therefore, much more likely to be real and open to healing. Natural beauty: the rustling of leaves in the trees and fast flowing streams, the vast expanse of the ocean and rolling green hills, can work wonders of healing for a broken heart. In a similar way, a weary mind or a tense body can feel its life return by feasting the eyes on a riot of blossoming roses or by just listening to birds singing.

A growing awareness of the cosmic Christ: the presence of God in all things, is the sure sign that the reality of the Resurrection is dawning in our lives. So strong was this for John of the Cross that he addresses his beloved Christ in the names of creation.[37]

"My Beloved is the mountains,
and lonely wooded valleys,
strange islands,
and resounding rivers,
the whistling of love-stirring breezes,
the tranquil night
at the time of rising dawn,
silent music,
sounding solitude,
the supper that refreshes and deepens love."

Now, however, it is time for us to go in the early light of dawn to that garden where, according to the Gospel story, an empty tomb points towards the Resurrection. We go with the woman who is among the first recorded witnesses to the risen Christ.[38]

7.9 Arise, My Love and Come!

In the Fourth Gospel no word is simply what it is, so we must discern the meaning of an event in the symbolic resonance of the words. The story of Mary Magdalene's encounter with the risen Christ is given by the Fourth evangelist (John 20:1-2 and 11-18). But the significance of the story gains from being prefaced by a passage from the great biblical love-song.

"Arise, my love, my fair one, and come away;
the winter is past, the rain is over and gone.
The flowers appear on the earth,
and the vines are in blossom...
My dove, in the clefts of the rock,
in the covert of the cliff,
let me see your face, let me hear your voice,
for your voice is sweet, and your face is lovely."
                                    (Song of Solomon 2:10-14)

In the love song there are levels of meaning and interpretation which make it rich in possibility for application, but one at least allows us to hear God, like the lover calling to the beloved. In the story of Mary Magdalene Jesus is certainly calling her to arise to a new kind of life, but this is possible because he himself has been called to arise by God, his Father, and all creation is seen to have arisen with him. Here is a celebration of the love that awakens to a new life and makes creation and every created being the beloved of God. The story spells out the truth step by step in a dance of recurring turnings that are really deep conversions for the heart.

Mary Magdalene makes her return to the tomb while it is still dark. If hope seems gone, Mary will still come back seeking the body of Jesus. Mary remembers Jesus as the man who knows her past and who, in forgiving her, gave her back to herself. For Mary, it is not just the Lord's body, but the Jesus who had loved and affirmed her who had been taken away. Mary's is not now the pain of failure or guilt. Her suffering is the pure pain of loss. The sense of loss is more inward and interior than the sense of failure or guilt. It pierces to the very core of being, to the sense of being loved, being valued and being given meaning. Mary knew that Jesus loved her from her first encounter because of the quality of his forgiveness. Then he had spoken her new name in her heart, and she had come to be again through his word.

Returning to the empty tomb, Mary goes back in her memory to her first 'turning back'. She remembers her conversion from her life as a public sinner, and again the tears begin to flow: tears of compunction in which deep sorrow for sin, longing desire and the passion of love flow together as one. It was the goad of God awakening her to his coming, even in his absence, like a spear opening the wound of love. The empty tomb echoed the hollow emptiness of her heart, sensing nothing but the pain of yearning. But she does not go away. She turns back again, and lingers by the empty tomb. Then she stoops to look into it. But still she weeps, and to the angel's question,

'Why are you weeping?'

she can only express her experience of loss,

'They have taken away my Lord,
and I do not know where they have laid him.'

(John 20:13)

But saying this, the evangelist underlines, 'she turned round'. She turns again: another conversion; and turning round, she sees Jesus as a stranger, the known in the unknown. But she does not give up. Like the lover in the Canticle, she goes on seeking (Song of Solomon 3:1-3).

Jesus appearing as the gardener, adds to the question of the angels, his own question,

'Whom are you looking for?'

(John 20:15)

To weeping for the death must be added seeking for the resurrection. Mary is ready to go on hoping for she knows not what, as she is ready for labour beyond her natural strength.

'Sir, if you have carried him away, tell me where you have laid him and I will take him away.'

(John 20:15)

She seeks Jesus with the whole of her being. She is, therefore, ready for his coming, and so she hears when Jesus speaks her name: 'Mary' (John 20:16).

Yet again, the evangelist underlines the movement, 'She turned.' This is a further conversion, simple but total. Mary addresses Jesus as 'Master'. All the experience of their

139

past relationship is made present in that word, and in the gesture that seeks to embrace Jesus. Again, the Canticle can give her the words,

> 'I have found him whom my soul loves.
> I held him and would not let him go.'
>
> (Song of Solomon 3:4)

Here the active passion of love and the passive passion of waiting meet as the fruit of her labour.

7.10 A woman's Witness: Go and Tell

Up to this point we are still in the context of the death of Jesus, but Mary Magdalene is teaching us a response that goes beyond loss and grieving. She returns, turns back, turns round, and turning, sees. While it was still dark, she draws upon the memory of where Jesus has been for her. She seeks and she asks. She refuses to accept that lostness is the end of the process. Her hope goes beyond hopelessness. Like a blade of grass pushing up beneath heavy concrete, relentlessly she seeks the light. Her faith, her hope and her love are all in the waiting. And in that blind stirring of love that is becoming a passionate living flame, resurrection's dawn is silently breaking through the innermost heart of her loss. Mary is not dead because Jesus is not dead.

The resurrection, however, is still coming. This is the mystery. There is yet another 'turning' for Mary, as Jesus implies by his response.

> "Do not hold on to me...
> I have not yet ascended to the Father;
> but go to my brothers and say to them,
> I am ascending to my Father and your Father,
> to my God and your God."
>
> (John 20:17)

Mary is not to cling to the knowing she already has of Jesus. There is more yet to come. She is being taken into communion with the Father as Jesus prepares to give her the life he shares with the Father in the Spirit: the best Comforter of all. No longer is Jesus to be simply with Mary in his humanity. The presence of the Spirit of Christ is to be within her. Now she must show in some small way that she has grasped not just the love story of Jesus and Mary but also the mystery of Jesus in Mary. She must, therefore, turn again, and turn back to where she had started, and know the place as for the first time, because now she knows it anew, in God. But then she must return, turn back again, and go and tell her story. She must give her 'confessions': the memory of the great things God has done in her from the beginning until this moment. She must bear witness, through the story of her own life, to God's saving love in her, and so lead others to Jesus. She has a message about Mary that is at heart a message, a gospel, about Christ. In Mary, the memory of the Passion becomes the Resurrection, as she bears witness in the process of the mission she has received: 'I have seen the Lord' (John 20:18).

Mary Magdalene is prepared to let go of the Jesus she had known in human form, to do what he had asked of her, going out into the future. Always we must seek and go beyond where we are, never resting. Now, becomes 'Passion' when we are called to go further. There, where he goes before us, is 'Resurrection'. Resurrection is a symbol of purification from what we can grasp, because God wants to give us more. In the garden of the Resurrection Mary has found the risen Jesus and received her new mission. Now she is to go and find the cosmic Christ everywhere and in all things, as she tells her story wherever she turns, yet again. For Mary has found a new freedom: the freedom of the Spirit; the Spirit of Christ within her.

7.11   *Freedom of Spirit*

Spirit of God, breathe now where you will
I am open now like the lotus flower,
open and silent, tranquil and still.
Spirit of God, here are depths deep to fill
I am waiting now like the lotus flower
for wisdom that love alone can distil.
Spirit of God, breathe like the wind through the
    grass and the corn;
dispel the thick cloud and streak the grey dawn.
Spirit of God let new life come to birth,
like the green shoot breaking hard crusted earth.
Fire and water, light and air, distilled drops of rain
    on the sea
cry aloud, again and again: I'm free!
For the Spirit has taken possession of me
and I'm awake to the light, and free – Just to be!

8.

Earthing the Vision

8.1 Reconciling the Past for Future Hope

Radiance belongs to the vision of faith that gives a sense of mission to life. But the vision still has to be earthed by being applied and lived out daily in a gradual process. This means that the past must be fully integrated into the present to give a sure foundation for the future mission. This process is focussed in another story of a resurrection appearance in which the disciples experience their reconciliation encounter with Jesus before he missions them for their future ministry (John 21:1-23).

A group of the disciples appear to be dejected, not knowing quite what to do after the death of Jesus. The only obvious thing seemed to be to return to what they knew how to do: fishing. Peter, as usual, takes the initiative and tells the others that he is going fishing, anyway. The others said they would go with him. What follows seems like a replay of Peter's call story early in Jesus' ministry, but now some of the lessons taught then, seem to have been learnt. The disciples were in the boat all night fishing, but they caught nothing. Their memories must have been alive even if they said very little: memories about their first enthusiastic following of Jesus; and then the shabby way in which they had deserted him when he was under attack. Peter's conscience was particularly heavy. The thought of his rejection of Jesus in words of denial tore at his heart and tears were always near the surface. A night in which he had again caught nothing could only remind him of other empty nights.

As the dawn began to break the disciples came towards

the shore of the lake. They were just looking, aimlessly, or so it appeared. Then a stranger seemed to emerge on the shoreline, and a voice called out asking if they had caught any fish. To their negative response came back the stranger's reassuring words, "Cast the net to the right side of the boat, and you will find some!" (John 21:6). The disciples, almost automatically, do what they are told, although they were scarcely able to haul in their great catch. But the response of the disciples was appropriate to each one.

The disciple who was close to Jesus at the disciples' farewell meal, just looked more intently at the shore. Loving and being loved, made him quick to recognise the apparent stranger. Tradition equates him with John Zebedee, one of the first disciples, but theology sees him also as an image of the true disciple of Jesus, loving and being loved, close enough to know the thoughts of his heart. Now, the fruit of his long contemplative look was to know the identity of the stranger, and so he tells Peter, "It is the Lord!" (John 21:7).

Peter's response is equally characteristic of his impulsive and generous nature. Inappropriately, it would seem, he put something on before he jumped into the lake. Meanwhile, the rest of the disciples dealt practically with the fact that they had a large haul of fish to be dragged in. They landed their catch because they were not far from land.

What greeted the disciples as they came ashore was a charcoal fire with fish being cooked and bread prepared: a welcome breakfast. But clearly there was more to it than breakfast! Peter kept himself busy with hauling the net ashore. The sight of a charcoal fire might have been almost too much. Inevitably it would have reminded him of the night beside another fire on which he said he did not know Jesus. But Jesus just welcomed them with the familiar word 'come' that always drew them to him, and with the characteristically practical invitation, "Come and have breakfast!" (John 21:12).

It was a warm but awesome moment for them all. Not one of them dared to ask him 'Who are you?' because they knew it was Jesus. They knew because they recognised the welcome of his love in such simple ways, such as the way in which Jesus came and took the bread and the fish and gave it to them. It was a moment of deep reconciliation, there by the lake of Galilee: the lake that could tell so many stories of stormy weather and calm after the storm, whether this referred to the seasons of nature or to the human heart that Jesus had touched.

8.2 Generous Love: the Foundation for Ministry

Peter, however, needed more than the rest. The other disciples had just not been around when Jesus could have expected their support. But they had not said anything. They had not said that they did not know Jesus. Peter knew that he had opened his mouth again and used his words to deny the one he loved so much. He needed to speak again. He needed to use words to articulate what he really felt. He needed to say he was sorry, however much he had wept his sorrow. Again, as always, Jesus knew his man. He knew what was in this human heart. Jesus staged the drama of Peter's rehabilitation (John 21:15-23). Three times Jesus asked Peter solemnly,

"Simon, son of John, do you love me?"

(John 21:16)

Recalling the three denials, Jesus was giving Peter the opportunity to make three affirmations of his love. On each of the first two occasions Peter replies,

"Yes, Lord, you know that I love you."

(John 21:16)

On both occasions Jesus simply responds by reaffirming the ministry that he had envisaged for Simon Peter from the beginning of their relationship. Peter would still be a fisher of men but he would also take on the pastoral care of others. Certainly Jesus had no intention of taking back the authority that he had invested in Peter. He still trusted him. But hearing Jesus' question for the third time, all the deep distress of Peter's past denial comes to the surface. With great anguish he opens up the whole truth of his grief before Jesus for understanding, forgiveness and healing.

> "Lord, you know everything; you know that I love you."
> (John 21:17)

In this moment Jesus gives Peter not only forgiveness and healing for the past but also the grace of future hope. Again he missions Peter for the pastoral care of those who would follow Jesus, and in doing so clarifies the basic qualification for that mission: the quality of love. In the same incident Jesus reminds us that love is what he needs from his disciples if they want to carry on his mission.

The story, however, has an epilogue which reminds us of the uniqueness of each disciple's call. Jesus begins to speak about Peter's future ministry and his martyr's death.

> "Truly, I say to you, when you were younger, you used to...go wherever you wished; but when you grow old, you will stretch out your hands, and someone else will... take you where you do not wish to go."
> (John 21:18)

Peter has to realise, as do all who commit themselves to be available for Christ's mission, that they may be led in ways not envisaged at the beginning of their commitment, because Christ is living his life through them for God's work on earth. But Peter demonstrated a characteristic that remains common among human beings. He turned aside and proceeded to ask what would happen to another disciple. Jesus firmly tells him that Peter's concern should not be in curiosity about the other. His calling lay in following

146

Jesus in the way that he had now been sent. His own personal vocation to follow Christ was the important thing for him, as it was for the other disciple. This is a word of direction that we often need to bring us back to the uniqueness of each person and so of each calling.

8.3 *The Lesson of the Lake*

The scene on the shore of the lake in Galilee reminds us, as it reminded the disciples, of the deepest lessons we need to learn: that we are loved by God; that love casts out fear; and that being unafraid to face the truth, the truth will set us free. Then we can begin to believe in the truth that the only essential gift God needs from us if we are to share in Christ's mission, is our love: at least our desire to want God and to be for God just as we are.

> I could see
> there in the lake
> the dance of the reeds,
> there in the water
> with ripple of laughter,
> slender and tall,
> rising and fall;
> there in the waves
> moving and still
> while joy had its fill,
> gracefully flowing,
> touching and knowing
> a tender caress,
> a breath, or just less
> of warm-feeling air.
>
> What intimacy!
> They were free
> and made one
> there in the sun

through the air,
just there
in the lake,
I could see.

Come, they said, Come!
Love, casting out fear
has drawn you near.
Come, they said, come!
Be set free and made one
in the Son
through the air:
God's Spirit, God's air.

Come, said the lake.
Let go,
then you'll know
it is I,
not water or sky.
Let God take.

Come, let the truth
rock with the waves.
Come, know the truth
that heals as it saves.
Come, let the truth itself
set you free
to love.

What intimacy
God's loving can be!
The whole lake could see
the waves rocking me,
setting free
the God that's in me
to love.

8.4 Reflecting Together: An Emmaus Walk

Keeping alive the memory of our call as we become involved in earthing Christ's mission, is vital both for our sense of urgency and our trust. In a gem of a resurrection story Luke's Gospel provides us with two modes of remembering that make this a present and life-giving reality. Jesus appears disguised as a stranger joining two rather depressed disciples on their way to the village of Emmaus, about seven miles outside Jerusalem. The narrative holds more than might appear. Through the medium of the story, Luke is trying to tell us about the ways in which the risen Christ is present through his Spirit among those who have faith (Luke 24:13-35).

The two disciples, obviously without much faith and even less hope, were talking together as Jesus gradually drew near and then joined them. Like any good counsellor or friend, Jesus had discerned their mood and began by asking them a question which would enable them to talk. He asked them about the subject of their conversation which so obviously preoccupied them. The two disciples were clearly surprised that he did not know. They suggested that he must be a visitor since he appeared to be ignorant of recent events in Jerusalem. Jesus encouraged them to tell him what had happened, while he listened. The story came out with its sad facts, and their feelings about them. They told him how Jesus of Nazareth, whom many had hailed as a prophet, had been put to death by their religious and civil authorities. Then came the punch line: the source of their dejection,

"We had hoped that he was the one to redeem Israel. Yes, and besides all this, it is now the third day since these things took place. Moreover, some women of our group astounded us. They were at the tomb early this morning and did not find his body."

(Luke 24:21-22)

Jesus let them get through the details that confused and upset them. Then he chided them gently, gradually enabling hope to seep through their hopelessness, as he related all they knew about the word of God in Scripture to their experience of Jesus in their own lives.

"O how foolish you are and how slow of heart to believe all that the prophets have declared! Was it not necessary that the Christ should suffer these things and then enter into his glory?"

(Luke 24:25-26)

In this way Jesus was helping them to reflect upon their own lives in the light of the word of God as it was interpreted by Jesus. Death and resurrection could then be seen as part of the rhythm of life, both for Christ and those who believed in him. We learn this by reflecting upon our lives in the light of the Jesus story. We may not see the presence of God in the present moment as it happens, but as we reflect upon what has happened, we are given a certain sight of God as we listen and discern God's voice in all that has come to us. In hindsight we are given insight, which then becomes foresight for our future.

If we go on to share our reflection with another, we mutually support each other's faith and make it come alive, as we find words to articulate our experience. Then we appreciate the reflection of the disciples at Emmaus,

"Were not our hearts burning within us
while he was talking to us on the road..
opening the Scriptures to us?" (Luke 24:32)

8.5 The Breaking of the Bread

The disciples were nearing the village of Emmaus. Their step was lighter. Now they were only anxious that they might lose their new companion on the way, as it seemed he intended to go on further, so they persuaded him to remain with them.

> "Stay with us, because it is almost evening,
> and the day is nearly over."

(Luke 24:29)

Jesus complied with their wishes and went in to stay with them. Then came the moment of recognition. When Jesus was at table with them, he took the bread and blessed, and broke it, and gave it to them. At that moment their eyes were opened. But as soon as they recognised him, Jesus seemed to vanish from their sight.

The painter Rembrandt captured the immediacy of this moment in a study of light. Pools of light focus upon the face of Jesus and the broken bread in his hands. Light makes them one, with a significance that belongs to the presence of Jesus in the broken bread. This moment is about the immediacy of the risen Christ who always comes in some way as a surprise: sudden in his appearing. But it is also about the way in which the risen Christ remains for us under the appearances of a meal in bread and wine, to build communion out of the community of those who dare to believe.

8.6 Do This in Memory of Me

Before he died, Jesus gathered up the meaning of his life and death in a symbolic gesture at a farewell meal for his closest disciples. The apostle Paul captures its significance, by the way in which he hands on the tradition of this seemingly timeless moment. He writes to the early Christian community in Corinth by way of clarification.

> "I received from the Lord what I also handed on to you; that the Lord Jesus, on the night when he was betrayed, took a loaf of bread, and when he had given thanks, he

151

broke it and said, 'This is my body, that is broken for you. Do this in remembrance of me.' In the same way, he took the cup, also after supper, saying, `This cup is the new covenant in my blood. Do this, as often as you drink it, in remembrance of me.' For as often as you eat this bread and drink this cup, you proclaim the Lord's death until he comes."

(1 Corinthians 11:23-26)

So much psychic and physical energy is wasted damming up the pain of the past. Only remembering the past, as our memory gives it to us in the present, can truly liberate us for the future. Memory of the past is a mysterious key opening on to the future, but its power lies in its capacity to make present. At the moment of his farewell meal, Jesus was acting out what he wanted to be our gesture of remembrance in the future, looking back at his past life and death. When he took bread, and blessed, and broke it, he wanted our memory to make present the past of his life and death, with its unique power to heal and save. When he took the cup of wine, he wanted us to remember his suffering in the outpouring of his blood in death and to recognise and claim its life-giving power. Jesus knew and wanted us to know, that this was a uniquely powerful event in which, literally, remembering the past of his Passion, we could be set free from the burdens of our past, until the fullness of the cosmic presence of Christ became a reality in the future.

Jesus' gesture with the bread and wine, however, was not just his gift for our remembrance and re-enactment. It was a gift in which all humanity and all creation were involved in giving as well as receiving. The bread and wine are symbols, both on the physical and on the psychic level. There is a cultural process involved, which reaches from the cultivated earthy fruits to the cuisine that prepares a meal for nourishment and celebration. They are fruits of the earth and work of human hands: integral to our culture. They can, therefore, realistically represent the offering of our world and ourselves: creation and creativity, to God.

But there is more to the symbolism. The grain is from the dying seed but with the yeast its rising forms the bread. The vine's grape is crushed and its fermentation intoxicates the grape-juice for wine that heals and delights the spirit. The processing of bread and wine, therefore, is a powerful symbol of the dying and rising Christ. Our offering, then, is taken up into Christ's. It is the meal that creates a sacred space for thanksgiving. Here true community is formed in a sharing of bread and wine that represents our lives and becomes Christ. Here is found a hearth and the heart of a real holy communion in spirit and in truth.

8.7 God as Food For the Hungry

It is not by chance that Jesus spoke about the joys of heaven and earth in terms of a banquet or a wedding feast, and seemed to spend much of his time at meal celebrations. Food seemed to speak to him of human bonding, and the wine that flowed was a reminder of that priceless quality of relatedness between human beings. So at the end of his life Jesus chose our most fundamental need of food to be the effective sign of God's presence not only with us but within us in all our human need. There is no closer sign of intimacy than that imaged by the consumption of food that is changed within us into our body's substance. Perhaps only the starving, those who know real hunger and thirst, can appreciate what it means to say that God chose to come and remain with us as food. It demonstrates God's love for all creation: a love that desired an ever deeper sharing of life. This was what Jesus imaged in the parable of the vine and its branches.

> "Abide in me as I abide in you.
> Just as the branch cannot bear fruit by itself
> unless it abides in the vine,
> neither can you, unless you abide in me."

(John 15:4)

The fruit he wanted was the transformation of the world through love. Hence the imperative,

> "Abide in my love."
>
> (John 15:9)

The evidence suggests that so ordinary a sign was not readily accepted by those who heard Jesus say,

> "I am the bread of life.
> Whoever comes to me will never be hungry.
> Whoever believes in me will never be thirsty."
>
> (John 6:35)

It still asks for the kind of faith that was the response of the disciples for whom Peter spoke.

> "Lord, to whom can we go?
> You have the words of eternal life."
>
> (John 6:68)

8.8 The Echo of the Empty Tomb

Apart from the stories of appearances of the risen Jesus, there is another resurrection tradition illustrated in the short ending of Mark's Gospel with a statement to three women about their discovery of an empty tomb (Mark 16:1-8).

> "Do not be amazed: you are looking for
> Jesus of Nazareth, who was crucified.
> He has risen, he is not here...
> Go, tell his disciples and Peter
> that he is going before you into Galilee.
> There you will see him."
>
> (Mark 16:6-7*)

Fear paralysed the women. They had remained with Jesus in his suffering and grieved after his death, but they could not move beyond the dead body and the empty tomb. They were confused and so they did not stay to seek any further, and seemingly they did not give any message but fled from the tomb trembling with astonishment.

The empty tomb remains a powerful theological image proclaiming the truth of the resurrection of Christ. It reminds us of the continuity that exists between the risen Christ and the humanity of Jesus as he had been known during his earthly life, and it tells us clearly that death and burial are not the end of that life's meaning. Equally, however, it reminds us, as do the resurrection appearance stories, that the manifestation of the risen Christ is not subject to the limitations of earthly existence with its need for sense perception. The Spirit of the risen Christ is an all-pervasive presence. To become aware of such a presence within all things, requires a cleansing of our perception of reality: a new kind of vision. It arises from a refusal to accept death as the ultimate end of life's process. The risen Christ is always coming into our lives. To believe this, regardless of apparent death and desolation, belongs to the new vision. But we still need the echo from the empty tomb as we try to earth the vision. It is significant for a life lived in faith.

The resurrection stories of the appearance of the risen Jesus to those who knew him before his death, have as their purpose the healing of the wounds of the past, so that each believer could feel secure in the context of a God who loves, and so look towards the future with hope and realism. But, as a resurrection symbol, the empty tomb, like the figure of the stranger in the appearance stories, takes us beyond familiar images and expectations. It speaks of the purification of our desires. Our ego likes to remain in control. When the resurrection grace is operative in our life, it de-centres the ego and allows the Spirit of Christ to direct us from within. This is growth towards inner freedom. It begins with the acknowledgement of our poverty and is open to wait for the truth that gradually liberates as it transforms a whole life-style. Having a vision and being

155

vulnerable go together. The empty tomb is waiting for that hollowing-out in us that will echo its own space. The empty space then reminds us that God is always beyond our concepts and imagination. It safeguards the need for transcendence and calls for our trust. God is not an object we can control, but is the reality we can ultimately trust.

8.9 *Into the Future: He is Going Before You*

The resurrection statement of the empty tomb is that 'He is not here.' But it has an important sequel. 'He is going before you' proclaims a risen Christ who is always leading us out and on into the future. This is the mystery of the adventure of life both here and beyond. As the risen Christ recedes into the horizon before us, he is drawing us home on a great return journey to the God whom he addresses, with us, as our Father. This is a call that takes us beyond fear to trust, because Jesus remains the way. We are moving always between the familiar and the unknown, but with and in the Spirit of one who knows.

The more the resurrection grace takes over, the more we shall be truly turned towards the future, for faith is sheer openness to the future. Any closure marks our fear. It is this bold kind of faith that Paul shares with us when he says,

> "but this one thing I do: forgetting what lies behind
> and straining forward to what lies ahead,
> I press on toward the goal of the heavenly call
>   of God in Christ Jesus."

(Philippians 3:13-14)

Gregory of Nyssa was fascinated by Paul's image of "straining forward". It inspired him to speak of being prepared for constant change: the conversion implied in continual growth. This for him, was the call of life both here and hereafter.[39] Ultimately the only serious sin is a refusal to grow. We need humbly to learn from our mistakes, but not to cling to remorse and misery. Each successive death, however it comes, will bring its resurrection. Every ending is a new beginning: the new creation emerging in us. Finding God consists in endlessly following Christ, seeking God as the reality that always lies beyond our grasp.[40]

Openness to the future measures our growth in the freedom of the Spirit. Trusting the movements of the Spirit guiding our life, we are more prepared to let go of the unnecessary baggage of our past life. A new simplicity is coming into our life. We are becoming more and more our own unique selves and are content to be just that, knowing that only so, can we reflect our likeness to Christ.

Christian prayer operates now in a way that reflects a growing awareness of the cosmic Christ. Rooted and grounded in Jesus in his historical reality, it responds to the fact that through his death and resurrection the body of Christ is in some mysterious way, universalised. We enter into a new relationship with the world as a dimension in which the risen Christ is present to us. Co-extensive with the universe, the cosmic Christ is truly present in all things.

The very extent of such a presence encourages us to accept the darkness of a seeming absence, as we realise the inevitable transcendence of God, even within the vast nearness of his cosmic presence. Silence and the empty space will speak of the mystery that lies beyond all our attempts to grasp it. We simply trust in the universal presence of the cosmic Christ, and take all creation and every human being with us in our prayer.

> "In prayer we come to him
> with everything that touches our life,
> with the sufferings and hopes of humanity.
> We learn to remain in silence
> and poverty of heart before him.
> In the free gift of ourselves
> we learn to adore and to abide in his love.

The Spirit dwelling within us
gradually transforms us, enabling us
through His power to remove whatever
hinders His action.
The Spirit unites and conforms us to Jesus
and makes us sensitive to His presence
within ourselves, in others and in all that happens.
Thus we learn to contemplate reality
and to experience it with His Heart,
to commit ourselves to the service of the Kingdom
and to grow in love."[41]

A resurrection person lives open to the universe because growth in the contemplative spirit implies a development towards cosmic consciousness. Contemplative persons simply take on the mind and heart of the cosmic Christ and let Christ pray in them through the Spirit to the Father. This is Trinitarian prayer. It is also prayer for the world.

8.10 All in the Waiting

The Spirit of Christ does set us steadfastly turned towards the future. But we cannot fly to the horizon that draws us onwards. Time stretches out before us and we have to live within it and use it as a precious commodity given to us moment by moment. Only small steps, possible goals and steady progress will lead us to what our vision has glimpsed. Nothing remains the same: everything changes, both circumstances and our moods. This can be a source of constant encouragement to be and to do. But it can also bring a corresponding temptation to nurse feelings of doubt about ourselves, and fears related to our sense of inadequacy. Just to wait and bide time, to be patient with what is, and most of all with ourselves, is the most difficult task for any human being. We constantly need to learn the lesson of waiting. For, as T.S. Eliot tells us, the faith and the love and the hope are all in the waiting.[42]

The vicissitudes of light and shade belong to every stage of our spiritual journey but they are for our growth in anxiety-resisting trust. As one mystic images the process, God wants us to become as spiritually supple as a soft leather glove to the hand.[43] But it is Julian of Norwich who puts her finger on the root cause of our doubt and fear when she stresses that what most hinders growth in those who want to love God is their failure to really trust in God's love for them.[44]

The ongoing message for our life in Christ, therefore, is clearly, one of patience and trust. It asks for a response that is eminently possible because it rests upon the truth that God is love and that he loves us.

We are not to pretend that our wounds are not there. Acknowledgement and acceptance are part of the process of healing. But neither are we to concentrate on the wounds. Instead we are to look on the healing love of Christ and our true self held deeply in God. Moreover, although it is unwise to ignore our feelings, they must not become the sole criterion by which we judge reality because inevitably our feelings fluctuate and so remain unreliable as guides to the whole truth. Rather, our discipline must be in training ourselves to focus on the truth of God's love for us, so that we find our security in God instead of nursing our negative feelings of depression and fear. God is ultimately a God of consolation who asks only for our faith, our hope and our love. It is this realisation that prepares us for the mission that is supremely ours as we continue to live in the Spirit of the risen Christ in our world.

9.

A Prophetic Mission: Compassion

9.1 A Mission to Love

We all have our visions and dream our dreams. They energise us and move us on into the future. But a vision remains a disembodied concept if it does not progressively transform life around where it has taken root, and shape it according to its inner purpose.

When in the Gospel we hear Jesus exclaim,

> "I came to bring fire to the earth
> and how I wish it were already kindled!"
>
> (Luke 12:49)

we know that he was energised by a sense of urgency that came from the immediacy of his own prophetic vision of the world. The image was of fire cast upon the earth. The reality was the Spirit of God who would empower those who believed in Jesus, to carry on his mission of love.

The vision that we have discovered in the heart of Christ is the vision of a world wounded and yet loved by God. But it comes with a mission to change the world. It is a vision therefore that still needs to be earthed through the justice that is effective love.

A prophet sees simultaneously, in a sudden moment of recognition, what is and what could be. Jesus knew that it was not enough simply to broadcast a message of love. He understood that in the real world of his day many suffered the unequal effects of the lack of loving compassion. He saw that many were oppressed by an unjust society structure that operated not out of love but from greed and possessiveness. These people were the poor.

Two consequences followed from this assessment. Such a society could not be transformed by love unless the balance were redressed in favour of the poor; and such a mission could only be achieved by a power of love that went beyond human capacity. It would need empowerment by the Spirit of love that was God's own.

9.2 *Empowered by the Spirit*

It was with this prophetic vision and concern that Jesus came to the synagogue in his home town of Nazareth. Here apparently was a simple itinerant preacher but in reality a living prophetic image of God, in the line of the great Jewish prophetic tradition, to speak to his own generation (Luke 4:16-30).

Luke, the evangelist, creates the drama of an incident in which Jesus unrolls the scroll of Isaiah and finds the place where it was written,

> "The Spirit of the Lord is upon me, because
> He has anointed me to bring good news to the poor.
> He has sent me to proclaim release to the captives,
> recovery of sight to the blind,
> and to let the oppressed go free."
>
> (Isaiah 61:1-2 in Luke 4:18-19)

Jesus then rolls up the scroll, gives it back to the attendant and sits down. The eyes of everyone are fixed on him as he shocks his hearers with the announcement,

> "Today, this Scripture has been fulfilled
> in your hearing."
>
> (Luke 4:21)

The response was very appreciative of Jesus' preaching, which was quite unlike that given by the normal run of scribes and Pharisees. But there the fascination with Jesus stopped. His audience was not prepared to have this word applied to them. It was fine so long as Isaiah remained beautiful poetry, but as a challenge that might change their lives, that was another matter. Their response was to try and get rid of Jesus. It was not comfortable listening to him because it obviously did mean conversion: a complete change of lifestyle.

Later Luke links the story with a message sent to ask whether Jesus was the Christ. Jesus sent back the messengers with another reference to prophecy,

> "Go and tell what you have seen and heard:
> the blind receive their sight, the lame walk,
> the lepers are cleansed, the deaf hear,
> the dead are raised, and the poor
> have the good news brought to them.
> Blessed is anyone who takes no offence at me."
>
> (Luke 7:22-23)

This was nothing more than a repeat of the Nazareth proclamation. The criterion by which the identity of Jesus, as the Christ, could be discerned was that of a mission to the poor, that is, to all who were in need.

9.3 Good News for the Poor

The poor, however, did understand something of what Jesus was saying. Jesus spoke of good news for the poor along with liberation of the oppressed. This could not but articulate their own desire to live as fully human beings, because they knew by experience the day to day injustice of an occupied people. They understood that Jesus, inspired and empowered by the Spirit of God, was speaking about justice in a society structured so that all might live to the full potential of their freedom. They saw this as God's vision that Jesus wanted to see actualised on earth.

But the poor also heard another message that forced

them to reflect upon how this could be achieved. Jesus had spoken about loving the enemy and doing good instead of taking revenge for evil inflicted. Violent insurrection, therefore, was not the obvious way of achieving justice. The way of non-violence suggested by Jesus was more rigorous, requiring personal conversion as integral to social change as well as courage, commitment and perseverance. It included individual soul-searching to recognise the deviance of the human heart that could project personal hurts on to social issues as a means of avoiding love's justice and compassion.

There was, however, an added dimension to Jesus' message. It meant realising that in the very simplicity of the life of the poor there was a certain affinity with the thrust of Jesus' words proclaiming that the poor in spirit were the truly blessed and happy (Matthew 5:3). Jesus wanted his hearers to understand that the poor in spirit, all those who lack and long for something, are in a real sense, open and empty, and so, ready to be filled. They are not encumbered by excess baggage or weighed down by a web of entangling material concerns. There is, in their hearts, a space for as yet unknown spiritual riches of being and not just of having. This potential for freedom of spirit had to be realised by the poor, but also learnt by the worldly rich before there could be any effective earthing of Jesus' message of liberation for the oppressed. Values and attitudes would have to change, not just the balance of wealth.

God's way is not about everyone becoming materially rich or poor. It is about justice for all, that is only possible where loving compassion operates, always in favour of liberating anyone who is oppressed and, therefore, unable to live fully as a human being. Love holds the key and is the criterion by which any law is to be interpreted and applied (Matthew 22:37-40). But so also is sincerity. The mask of hypocrisy has to be exposed to the light of truth. Jesus castigated attention to legal minutiae at the expense of "weightier matters of the law" such as "justice, mercy and faith" (Matthew 23:23) and so took to himself the task of Israel's prophets in exposing the hypocrisy that conceals injustice under other names.

9.4 *Justice in a Prophetic Tradition*

Jesus was first seen in the mould of the Jewish prophetic tradition which provided him with a model. During the eighth and seventh centuries BC great prophets like Amos and Hosea, Isaiah and Jeremiah took on the task of unmasking hypocrisy in high places. A significant change had developed in the history of the Jewish people who had found their identity through the response of Moses to God's act of liberation. The oppression and exploitation of the poor came now from among their own Israelite people. Their own rich and powerful were now practising what their predecessors had experienced at the hands of their Egyptian oppressors in the time of Hebrew slavery. The economic affluence of a people, who had settled down in their much coveted land of Palestine, had led to political oppression and a state-manipulated religion that bore little resemblance to the moral values of the God it purported to worship.

So the cries of the prophets surged like ever-recurring waves against the entrenched bulwark of privilege and calculated exploitation of the poor and marginalised. Faced with this evil distortion of freedom, God stands in judgement as advocate on the side of the poor, the powerless and the needy. So the prophets were fearless in speaking out, echoing the voice of God because the quality of their moral conscience had been finely tuned by their personal knowing of God. Judgement was for those with power.

> "It is you who have devoured the vineyard,
> the spoil of the poor is in your houses.
> What do you mean by crushing my people,
> by grinding the face of the poor?"
>
> (Isaiah 3:14-15)
>
> "For scoundrels are found among my people...

they set a trap; they catch human beings...
they have become great and rich,
they have grown fat and sleek.
They know no limits in deeds of wickedness.
They do not judge with justice
the cause of the orphan to make it prosper,
and they do not defend the rights of needy."

(Jeremiah 5:26-28)

The anguish of God in his prophets is clearly aggravated by the fact that such inhuman behaviour was carried out by people who claimed to be God's own and still engaged in some form of ritual worship. God's disdain, however, for any form of ritual worship which is not grounded in the everyday practice of justice for the poor, the weak and the oppressed, rings out loud and clear in the preaching of the prophets.

"Even though you offer me your burnt offerings
I will not accept them...
Take from me the noise of your songs..."

(Amos 5:22-24)

Amos' message is echoed in that of Isaiah.

"Look, you serve your own interests on your fast
day and oppress all your workers...
Is not this the fast I choose: to loose the bonds of
injustice... and let the oppressed go free?
Is it not to share your bread with the hungry,
and bring the homeless poor into your house;
when you see the naked, to cover them and not
to hide yourself from your own kin?

(Isaiah 58:3,6,7)

The resounding note of indignation, however, gives way to the yet more plaintive sound of lamentation, when the prophet bemoans the desolation and injustice of war. No

165

passage has such power to describe the devastation of a nuclear explosion and its fall out, or the consequences of technological warfare, so well as Jeremiah's lament on the waste land.

> "I looked on the earth, and lo, it was waste and void
>   and to the heavens, and they had no light.
> I looked on the mountains, and lo, they were quaking,
>   and the hills moved to and fro.
> I looked, and lo, there was no one at all
>   and all the birds of the air had fled.
> I looked, and lo, the fruitful land was a desert,
>   and all its cities were laid in ruins."
>
> (Jeremiah 4:23-26)

It is such war-torn waste lands that become the breeding ground of famine, so that the hunger trail of refugees joins those who are deported by force. God is present in the anguish of the exiled refugee, longing for the day of return to the remembered homeland of all such lost and listless peoples; but also in their cry for justice still. As in the prophet's song of the lover's vineyard, God looked, and still looks for justice but sees only bloodshed. God looked and looks for just relationships but hears only a cry (Isaiah 5:7).

A spirituality, implying a relationship to God, without justice, is an anachronism because justice is about right relationships. Justice remains an image of God and the criterion by which we can assess not only our response to God, but also our very knowledge of God. Humanity is itself a true image of God to the extent that it is moving always in the direction of reconciliation and peace among human beings. The foundation of such a movement is justice.

166

9.5 We Shall be Judged on Love

Jesus made the prophetic teaching on the primacy of practical love his own, and nowhere is this more clearly illustrated than in his parable that deals with the way in which human beings will ultimately be judged.

In the parable of the sheep and the goats, the exercise of judgement is about separating people, and the criterion by which they are separated is that of compassionate love. We shall be judged on love: human beings' humanity or inhumanity for each other (Matthew 25:31-46). At the end of their lives many may well be surprised at the way in which their caring concern for others is valued and so will ask,

> "Lord, when was it that we saw you hungry and
>   gave you food,
> or thirsty, and gave you something to drink?
> When was it that we saw you a stranger and
> welcomed you, or naked and gave you clothing?
> When was it that we saw you sick or in prison and
> visited you? "

(Matthew 25:37-39)

But they will receive the answer,

> "Truly, I tell you, just as you did it
> to one of the least of these who are members
> of my family, you did it to me."

(Matthew 25:40)

Because Jesus will take as being done to him whatever is done to anyone in need.

9.6 The Good Samaritan

This was the point of Jesus' justly famous parable of the good Samaritan given in reply to a lawyer who asked him to make it clear exactly who was his neighbour.

On a notoriously dangerous route from Jerusalem to Jericho, a man was stripped, robbed and beaten by robbers who left him half-dead. The scene remains alarmingly familiar. Two religious authority figures, a priest and a levite, passed by on the other side of the road, doing nothing for the wounded man. They did not want to get involved. But then a Samaritan, to the Jews a religious schismatic and therefore, an outsider, reached the spot where the injured man lay. Seeing him, the Samaritan not only tended the man's wounds, but took him to the nearest inn so that he could be nursed, while promising to return and deal with any additional expenses (Luke 10:29-37).

The teaching is as searching and relevant as it was in Jesus' own time. We can recognise the characters. Like the lawyer, we know who is the neighbour in the story: the one who had compassion. We do not need a commentary. We just need to absorb the story's truth about the cost of real compassion that is love in action. Our neighbour is an all-inclusive humanity. Social class, racial colour, religious creed, male or female, old or young, good or bad: the differences make no difference when it comes to our response. What unifies all these categories is the need of the individual person. The love that God asks of human beings is a love which responds to human need in the present moment. This is love's justice.

If we have learnt the lesson of the parable of the prodigal father, we shall understand the message of the good Samaritan. Ultimately, love's justice can only mean compassion. The two parables stand one at the beginning and one at the end of our pilgrimage. In between is a world wounded and yet loved by God.

9.7 A Passion for Justice

It was his passion for justice rooted in the compassion of God that ultimately brought Jesus to the incident that set the seal upon his death. The incident stands as a powerful image of Jesus' mission (Mark 11:15-19). Jesus had entered the outer court of the Jerusalem temple where the commercial transactions took place in preparation for the sacrifices used in worship in the temple. There appeared to be some legitimacy in what was going on. But Jesus knew well how easily buying and selling could result in a spin off of cheating, undercutting and downright robbery that had nothing to do with justice and fairness for those who could afford little. His anger at what he saw was obvious. He drove out those who were buying and selling and overturned the tables of the money-changers, and would not allow anyone to make a short cut carrying anything through the temple precincts. He saw that what was meant to be a house of prayer for all nations had been made a den of thieves (Jeremiah 7:11).

Aware of his radical concern for the poor and the outcast as integral to God's justice, as well as being asked to learn from Jesus because he was meek and humble of heart, we might well pause, perhaps puzzled, at the image of Jesus cleansing the temple. The significance of the incident, however, is considerable both on the level of the actual event and because of its symbolic value. Its immediate effect was climactic for the religious and civil authorities. It underlined for them that Jesus was a trouble-maker. He stirred things up. They were afraid of Jesus because the crowds remained fascinated by him and astonished at his teaching. After this the chief priests and the scribes looked for a way to destroy him. Jesus' suffering, imprisonment, trial and death began with this moment. The enemies of Jesus had long been waiting for their opportunity. The cleansing of the temple gave it to them.

So public an action in the place that focussed on the centre of the religious, political and social life of Jerusalem, enabled Jesus to demonstrate what was for him the most important reality in life.

The temple of Jerusalem was the house of God. It was a sign of the presence of God on earth. It was a way of recognising the reality of God at the heart of all creation. It gave a central focus to God: a sacred space. Not to treat this space with reverence, suggested that God was no longer really adored in spirit and in truth.

In practice, however, Jesus knew that the dynamic power of God's presence found its true temple only when it became an earthed reality in right relationships between human beings treating with each other in justice and love. It was human beings who were meant to be the living stones of the real house of God. To flout justice and to disregard compassion in the ordinary dealings of men and women was tantamount to practical atheism. Avowed belief in God was a mockery in the face of injustice. Jesus epitomised the truth he believed and lived, therefore, in a symbolic action that could not be missed. He proclaimed the breaking in of God's kingdom: God's way of justice in right relationships.

Meekness is power controlled, but it is power. Jesus was not afraid to use this power when it was a question of his supreme passion for God and God's justice. The climax of his sermon on the mount provides the words that are echoed in the actions of this incident:

> "Strive first for the kingdom of God and its justice."
> (Matthew 6:33*)

It is an appropriate climax to the teaching of Jesus. He wants all his followers to learn from the true meekness of his heart, how to share in his unwavering commitment to build up the kingdom of God on earth in justice and peace. In him the disciples of Jesus recognised the true prophetic servant of God.

> "Here is my servant whom I uphold,
> my chosen in whom my soul delights.
> I have put my Spirit upon him;
> he will bring forth justice to the nations.
> He does not cry or lift up his voice,
> or make it heard in the street;

a bruised reed he will not break,
and a dimly burning wick he will not quench...
He will not grow faint or be crushed
until he has established justice on earth."

(Isaiah 42:1-4 quoted in Matthew 12:18-21)

9.8 Compassion: Love's Justice

Justice for each person is important because God loves. But God goes beyond what is asked of human beings in the compassion that is love's justice. The image that the prophet Hosea paints for us is of a God of tenderness and compassion. Seeing the people of Israel in the image of a much loved child, Hosea speaks of God's steadfast love enduring throughout Israel's long and wayward story, mingling image and reality as he moves from the singular of the child to the plural of the people.

"When Israel was a child I loved him...
I took them in my arms;
but they did not know that I healed them.
I led them with cords of human kindness
with bands of love...
I bent down to them and fed them."

(Hosea 11:1,3,4)

But God suffers real pain of heart at the unfaithfulness of his own people that is in reality a failure to love.

"How can I give you up?
How can I hand you over?
My heart recoils within me,
my compassion grows warm and tender...
for I am God and no mortal,
the Holy One in your midst."

(Hosea 11:8-9*)

171

The words and the image are of one who is intimately and physically moved at the core and gut level of being, so that love literally hurts. But because God is bound to creation by love, the desire of God can only be for a kind of loving that is just and a kind of justice that is loving. Like the prophet, this means asking for a compassion that reflects God's own, so that as we walk humbly with God, we will learn to love tenderly and act justly (Micah 6:8).

10.

A Kind of Loving for Humankind

10.1 Kindness

Christ's mission to love has many facets and movements appropriate to each person's needs and stages of growth, but always it explores and extends our capacity for love to where the frontiers of the human open into God.

When Jesus asked his disciples to love one another as he had loved them, he introduced them to a quality of love which reflected the life of God because Jesus loved them as his Father, God, loved him (John 13:34 and 15:9).

Kindness is one of the easiest ways of making love known and of experiencing it and of preparing the way for others to understand the real truth about God. Kindness breaks down barriers where words may only make them and it is kindness that seems to characterise the non-judgemental attitude that Jesus affirms with such vivid images,

"Why do you see the speck in your neighbour's eye but do not notice the log that is in your own eye? In everything do to others as you would have them do to you."
(Matthew 7:3,12)

Perhaps it is not surprising, therefore, that we should find valuable insight into this kindness, in the very word itself. Love is essentially what God is. It is defined by the way in which the persons of the Trinity live in relation, so that they are one in their being. Because God creates our nature, he shares something of this characteristic, as potential within our nature. We are meant to be loving because we are created in the image of God. It is implied, therefore, that if we do not love, we do not really know God.

> "Let us love one another, for love is from God,
> everyone who loves... knows God...
> for God is love."
>
> (1 John 4:7-8)

It is the original double meaning contained in the fourteenth century development of the English word 'kindness', however, which gives us at the end of the twentieth century, a spiritual insight. The term 'kynde', from the Anglo-Saxon, had to do with 'nature' as the modern English speaks of 'human nature' as 'human kind'. This meaning remains in the modern English noun 'kind' meaning a species of nature. At the same time, the fourteenth century term belonged to 'goodness', and 'courtesy' or being 'good-hearted'. This meaning has survived in the modern English adjective 'kind' which means good, gentle and courteous.[45]

On account of this linguistic richness, Julian of Norwich can say that God is the very thing called kindness.[46] Kindness belongs to the very being of God. 'God's kind is to be kind', is how her teaching could be expressed for us, with a deliberate ambiguity trying to convey the reality of the nature of God as love. From this it follows that a kind person is not only like God, kind and loving, showing courteous goodness, but also one who is living according to human nature as it was intended in our creation. Our true nature is somehow hidden in the nature of God. It is for us to become true to our nature. Our growth would then be seen by our loving kindness. Unkindness is, in this way, both unkind and unnatural. It obscures what God would have us be. As Paul reminded an early Christian community, love is patient and love is kind (1 Corinthians 13:4). It is the visible sign of Christ-likeness proclaiming the fulfilment of a promise that a new heart will be given to us (Ezekiel 36:26).

10.2 Love: Sexuality and Spirituality

By our human nature we are designed as part of a whole so that we need each other. We are meant to be a network of loving and learning to love. But love touches every aspect of the human person so it is not possible to speak about love without raising the question of the relationship between sexuality and spirituality.

The experience and the frustration at the present stage of human evolution seem to be clamouring for a recognition of the spiritual dimension in love and so of sexuality. There is diffidence and difficulty in articulating an intuition that derives from experience, but the belief is growing that in human beings sexuality is meant to be an expression of the spiritual dimension of love that reaches beyond the body but is yet operative within and through the body. In terms of spirituality this can be understood by seeing the body as a revelation of the spirit.

The future of such a reflection on our sexuality lies in the character of wholeness that belongs to mature loving. In our present culture there is so much emphasis upon genital sex that we are in danger of giving insufficient consideration to other forms of intimacy. To say this, is not to undervalue the expression of genuine love through genital sex. Rather it is to emphasise its appropriate truth and responsibility. It will always hold the potential of creative and unitive love. This is God's gift and human delight for celebration but it operates most effectively as a maker of love in the context of ongoing faithful commitment because time is a womb of wholeness. It enables healing and engenders growth for both the persons involved and the new life that may issue from their union. But what of other forms of intimacy through which our personal sexuality may express genuine love?

1.3 The Art of Intimacy

We have had prophets for our times. Two merit mention in this context. Marie-Louise Von Franz, the Jungian analyst, referring to the fact that sexual freedom had been achieved by the last half of the twentieth century, went on to say that now we had to face the greater problem of liberating the heart. This she saw as the programme of the next fifty years.[47] The other prophet, the poet Rainer Maria Rilke, seems to parallel the challenge with a poetic line claiming that the work of sight had been done, so that it only remained for us to do heart work now.[48]

Doing heart work, for Rilke, would give rise to a new vision of love and a new mode for its expression. It would mean reverencing the relationship between two human beings as human beings, without putting the focus upon their sex. For Rilke this seemed to imply a love that was more human because it chose to protect the unique solitude of each person with a considerate gentleness, even while reaching out into that mysterious relating that belongs to the essence of love.[49]

Two phrases, in particular, carry the prophetic dimension because they point to future growth. The love is to be a more human love and to achieve it, we need to do heart work now, with an emphasis upon both 'heart' and 'work'. To bring this evolutionary possibility to fruition, we need those who will humbly take risks, accepting the discipline of pioneers, so as to explore with sincerity and longing the height and depth of love hidden in the relating of intimacy. There are no slick and easy answers. It is difficult, even perilous terrain but worth it for those drawn to the mystery of true ecstasy. But to arrive, such an adventure must be open to God, because God is love and it is God's Spirit of love who operates in this eminently spiritual work.

That the journey of exploring love should be begun, is almost inevitable. For we all need love and some measure of intimacy in relating, for our growth. But it will take courage and need encouragement to sustain the journey, because of the inevitable failures on the way. It follows, therefore, that we all need to learn how to create intimacy and how to cope with it. It doesn't always just happen, although the occasion for it may. Intimacy is an art: the art of communication and communion. All this leads us to focus upon our affectivity with its feelings and emotions seeking appropriate modes of expression.

Our sexuality operates in a more diffuse way through our affections. It gives a certain texture of warmth to our relating and so enables the flowering of trust. All this is the necessary threshold for intimacy. But, that intimacy in relating is an art, we soon realise as we make our mistakes. It requires a loving discernment to know how to speak and when to keep silence; as it does to know how to listen and when not to hear. Equally to know what to see and how to look, reveals a contemplative openness to truth and consistent sincerity in living. But to know how and when to use the language of touch is a refinement of art that calls for delicate intuition. If, however, we are to relate with wholeness and to facilitate wholeness in another, these are the lessons that we need to learn gently but surely for the sake of love and growth.

10.4 A Touch of Tenderness and Truth

We need words and gestures to facilitate the trust that makes for intimacy. But truth in relationships demands that our words and our gestures be unambiguous. this means that we are taken back to the intention that lies behind the action, and our responsibility for the way in which an expression of feeling could be received or interpreted. Clearly we shall fail in this area as in others. But hope is to be found in being clear about what we sincerely intend, as well as what we really want. The important thing here as elsewhere, is to learn and to grow through our experience.

Genuine loving affection always includes reverence and respect as well as warmth and wholeness in its mode of expression. We have, therefore, to try to create a space of loving reverence for intimacy. The key word in the process is 'space'. Space allows another to be. It recognises and accepts the otherness of the person, and the mystery of the human heart that is always a sacred space because it is the centre of love.

It is in such a context of space and closeness that touch has its meaning: a touch of tenderness and truth. Touch has the capacity to diffuse love in a sense of wholeness and healing. A warm hug can give security and a safe place for a tongue to unlock and tears to flow. A gentle touch of tenderness can relax and create peace as it quietly stills anxiety and tension. In grief and anguish it speaks more eloquently than words which can sound so hollow in moments of desolation. Touch can facilitate healing and forgiveness. But it can also enhance the intimacy of contemplative awareness and so give a realisation of God present and alive in human relating as sheer joy and ecstasy of loving. This is a hallowed space where love itself teaches us the reverence of letting go and letting be. Here two solitudes become sensitive to the space that lies between persons. While protecting each other's uniqueness, each is considerate of how and when to touch and greet the other. This is heart work: a sign of that freedom of the Spirit which transfigures the body, as the heart centres its life. The glow radiates to create a yet wider communion for all who still need loving.

10.5 The Taming of Friendship

Expressions of intimacy find a maturing growth in the love of friendship. Friendship is both a gift and an art of love that scarcely bears analysis, but it points towards a peak in human intimacy within all kinds of relationship. It involves a kind of loving in which heart work is paramount. So it requires the patient process of taming. This is the beautifully expressed message of Saint-Exupéry's story of the little prince.[50] In his conversation with the fox, the little prince learns that taming means to establish ties, which is a work of the heart, since it is only with the heart that we can see rightly. He learns, therefore, that taming means taking time to look, to listen and to wait upon the other, all of which belong to the journey of friendship. For friendship thrives and rejoices in allowing and wanting the other to be other, because of the joy of discovering the uniqueness of each person in the gradual process of time.

"The territories of friendship are not mapped.
You do not plan the journey, it is made
by moving, day after day,
into an unknown land.

No chart first guided you to thread its guardian seas.
This landfall came to you as though by chance,
wind and tides propitious, soundings clear.
But when you beached it was on friendly sands you
     leapt ashore,
a growing confidence and joy compelled your steps,
wondering if you slept, so dreamlike and so comforting
     it felt
along this new and unexpected way.

Towards what beckoning heights, mysterious,
     unscaled,
dark with the sombre secret of their forests, pure
in their crowning snows,
will these paths insist on taking you?
Over what unplumbed depths, what still, dark-watered
     lakes
will you be called to venture?

Sunlight itself, reflected goldmeal, blinding
in splintered gleams, making the joy
well-nigh unbearable, or shadows, rock-cold,

challenging a new-born trust, as yet untried,
must turn by turn colour your journeying.

The territories of friendship are not mapped.
Not that you are the first to travel in this land,
You are no pioneer along an unblazed trail
but rather one, neither the first nor last, of many
who rejoice that they are carried by this road;
who in the sacramental light of each new dawn
    have seen
the boundaries of the country wider spread,
have watched new valleys drink the shadows of the
    moving clouds,
fresh peaks rise up beyond the former skyline.

Many have passed along this way, have halted,
    evening come,
to view spread out below the ever-widening prospect
of their golden world. But they keep silence;
    this territory
is not won with guides, each for each self must find
    the way
and enter step by step
into the promised land.

It is a lonely and a solitary quest, you cannot show me
nor can I lead you, and yet we travel on it side by side.

The territories of friendship are not mapped.
The journey's made
by moving day after day
into an unknown land."[51]

10.6 Spiritual Energy Conservation

Our consideration of sexuality and spirituality thus far
has steadied its focus on the heart. This has been deliberate

because every human being, regardless of sex, age or particular calling, needs to give and receive the love of intimacy and friendship, at least in some measure, if there is to be growth to human maturity.

This has become a necessary prophetic emphasis as we near the end of the century which has prided itself on removing all sexual taboos. We know that not only freedom but physical and psychological sickness has come in the wake of greater sexual promiscuity. We need now not only to look with compassion and understanding at what is happening but to discern, through the expressed behaviour, the possibility of an unnamed desire for a new spiritual dimension of love waiting to emerge.

> Rising smoke obscures
> An open hearth fire within.
> Draw the flames upward!

This haiku suggests a new manifestation of the right ordering of love: the process that sees all our desires in relation to our ultimate desire. But we do well to ask questions about the experienced energy of our sexuality. The spiritual well-being of humanity is as much at stake as the health of the planet we inhabit.

Current thinking and experience has already moved towards a greater understanding of the role of sexuality in expressing love. But love and sexuality have as much to do with the art of human creativity in all its variety as with procreation and this itself suggests the significance of doing "heart work" now. There are signs that we need a further exploration of the spiritual dimension. The questions, if not the answers as yet, would seem to be taking us into an area that ecological concern for our planet has forced us to address. Energy conservation is the popular phrase on our lips as we move into the twenty-first century. It may be that this is precisely the way in which we need to reconsider our sexuality as we move towards 2000 AD, instead of applying piecemeal palliatives for what disturbs us.

181

Sexuality makes us aware of our separateness and yearn for our wholeness. Having sex is one of the ways in which we hope to ease the basic sense of aloneness. But even in the best of married relationships, the actual experience of union is always passing, so that, just because the relating is good, there will be an openness to that which still seems to lie beyond. This is because sexuality is about more than having sex. We are made for union and wholeness. We are made for love and intimacy, but of the kind that belongs beyond as well as within the human. The human satisfies us most when it is accepted for what it is: a foretaste, a human reflection of all that still remains in the potential of truth and love that is God. This is not to leave all the joy and ecstasy to a world beyond this. But it is to relate the two worlds as one. It is to see sexuality with all its potential for spirituality: a potential that so often seems to be wasted or left dormant. We still need to remember that God is love and draw upon God-power.

Teilhard de Chardin was one of the great prophets of the evolution of love and chastity in terms that come close to spiritual energy conservation. He spoke in prophetic language of his vision when he wrote,

"Physical union is already creating and nourishing a higher type of union in which the spiritual quality will eventually find realisation. Love is in the process of undergoing a change. In this new direction the human collective approach to God is being mapped out. Such a transformation of love will be accomplished once men and women feel the attraction of the divine personal centre drawing them to itself more strongly than a sexual attraction that might draw them prematurely to each other. What paralyses life, is the failure to believe and the failure to dare. Harnessing passion to make it serve the spirit must be a condition of progress. Sooner or later the world will take this step. Whatever is more true comes out into the open and whatever is better is ultimately realised. Some day after mastering space, the winds, the tides and gravity, we shall harness for God the energies of love. Then for the second time in the history of the world man will have discovered fire."[52]

Such a control implies first of all the harnessing of sexual energy, for the spiritual liberation of love. But harnessing presupposes the nurturing of love in reverence of persons and considerate tenderness. For divine love uses human love as a key to open our lives to the dimension of the spirit if we let it. Teilhard describes something of this initiation.

"A light glows for a moment in the depths of the eyes I love ... so fleeting, it was only that they might penetrate more deeply into my being, might pierce through to that final depth where the world itself had invaded my being. Under the glance that fell upon me, the shell in which my heart slumbered, burst open. With pure and generous love, a new energy penetrated into me or emerged from me that made me feel that I was as vast and as loaded with richness as the universe. Lord it is you who, through the imperceptible goadings of sense beauty, penetrated my heart in order to make its life flow out into yourself. You came down to me by means of a tiny scrap of created reality; and then suddenly unfurled your immensity before my eyes and displayed yourself to me as universal being."[53]

Teilhard is pointing towards a loving intimacy that is open to the Spirit and which becomes progressively transfigured by the presence of God. It is clearly a contemplative experience, full of wonder, that can be initiated by genuine human love. But he is suggesting that it is facilitated by a control and harnessing of sexual energy as something precious and valued and not to be used inappropriately or indiscriminately. It is such a vision which gives full value to both celibacy and marriage inspired by spiritual and Christian values.

Celibacy remains something of a travesty if it is not open to the vision of greater love. It belongs to the mysticism of love, not the legalism of law. To love widely and to be available for the mission of Christ in the world means loving more deeply. This means being open to intimacy with and in God. Lived then with courage and commitment, such a life will also be open to loving friendships where God's love creates new horizons of being, as the energy conserved enables a new spiritual creativity. Such a calling allows celibates to be pioneers in new modes of spiritual intimacy and living signs of our deepest desire: the yearning of our heart for the ultimate reality we call God.

True marriage is also founded upon the harnessing of sexual energy for genuine love, the creation of new life and the development of spiritual potential. Husband and wife commit themselves to a unique kind of fidelity and love towards each other which seeks to make their sexual union a sacred space for them alone. The potential for spiritual intimacy from so close a physical union is enormous if both partners can open their lives to the wonder of God's healing and creative love within them. Both husband and wife know in a radical way what it means to be exposed and vulnerable to another. But from mutual acceptance can grow a protectiveness and confidence that fosters self acceptance. They are called to be Christ to each other, so they need to be open to the ever greater coming of God into their lives in growing trust and love. Husband and wife are sexual partners but they are called to become soul mates, with a prophetic responsibility to share the love they find, that is of God.

It is not without significance that the author of a pastoral letter seeking to stimulate life in the spirit, should link together love, power and self-discipline. With such a combination of gifts bearing fruit, the spiritual transformation could have cosmic repercussions, capable of changing the world.

"Rekindle the gift of God within you.
For God did not give us a spirit of cowardice
but rather a spirit of power and love
and of self-discipline."

(2 Timothy 1:6-7)

10.7 God's Dream for the Earth

An attitude of considerate love inspired by an appreciation of energy conservation, will spill over into realistic concern for the earth. Phrases like 'virgin soil' and 'mother earth' remind us that we need to repent of the violence done to the earth by the rape of its resources for our own immediate gain. Genuine love will give us a new reverence for the earth and all creation. This is the message of those astronauts who have looked upon our planet from outer space.

"Seeing the earth for the first time I could not help but love and cherish her."[54]

"I realised that mankind needs height primarily to better know our long-suffering earth, to see what cannot be seen close up, not just to love her beauty, but also to ensure that we do not bring even the slightest harm to the natural world."[55]

"I was already aware of how small and vulnerable our planet is, but only when I saw it from space, in all its ineffable beauty and fragility did I realise that humankind's most urgent task is to cherish and preserve it for future generations."[56]

"Having seen the sun, the stars and our planet, you become more full of life, softer. You begin to look at all living things with greater trepidation ...and to be more kind and patient with the people around you."[57]

185

"I love looking on the earth. It isn't important whose she is, just that she is."[58]

Such words expose us to God's dream for the earth. For with Christ risen and rising in us from the tomb of the earth as from a womb giving birth, we are given a vision of a new creation, made new through Christ's mission of love.

"If anyone is in Christ there is a new creation,
everything old has passed away, see everything has
    become new
All this is from God, who reconciled us through Christ
and has given us the ministry of reconciliation."

(2 Corinthians 5:17-18)

Because of his faith in Christ, Paul's hope for the vision's ultimate realisation was certain in spite of all appearances to the contrary. But he was also aware of the urgency of the prophetic call for humanity's engagement in the service of reconciliation.

God's dream for the earth is communion: the full and free flowing of communication in the truth of the human spirit open to the Spirit of God. God is open to us but waits with gracious courtesy for each human being to be open to the presence of God within. Jesus echoed this desire with the words,

"Listen, I am standing at the door knocking;
If you hear my voice and open the door,
I will come in to you and eat with you,
and you with me."

(Revelation 3:20)

We have been learning from Jesus the art of loving but to do this effectively we also have to learn the art of being loved: the art of letting go and letting be and so of letting God love us. In the contemplative space of our heart we sit waiting for Jesus to knock at the door. When we open our heart to him, it is a moment of communion: the intimacy and immediacy of our presence to the presence of God. Then barriers can be broken down so that there are no boundaries. We are set free to see God's presence in all things and so build communion in an ever widening circle of community.

10.8 No Boundary

Love remains the voice of Christ's calling, releasing yet more love because there is no other way for the world to be transformed than by way of each individual's personal response, allowing love's radiance to proclaim 'no boundary.' The tree knew this truth when the rainbow touched its leaves. In moments of enlightenment the human heart senses it from within. From outer space astronauts of different nationalities have seen it so that they share in God's dream.

"From space I saw earth – indescribably beautiful with the scars of national boundaries gone."[59]

"The first day or so we all pointed to our countries. The third or fourth day we were pointing to our continents. By the fifth day we were aware of only one earth."[60]

"On the return trip home, gazing through 240,000 miles of space toward the stars and the planet from which I had come, I suddenly experienced the universe as intelligent, loving and harmonious."[61]

"Two words leaped to mind as I looked down on all this: commonality and interdependence. We are one world."[62]

No boundary
is real
as I stand
on the edge
of the world
reaching out.
It is sky
and I
am full
of the pull
of gravity
holding me
secure in the sun
and yet free.

Always
there is space
if I let go
of time
and let be
what is
in me.

In the earth
where I've trod
is God,
a heart's throb
pulsing life.

No boundary
is real
says the tree
to me.

11.

Epilogue:
A Mandala for the Heart

11.1 Wisdom of Heart

> "Through the vastness of creation
> Though your restless thought may roam,
> God is all that you can long for,
> God is all a creature's home."[63]

> "My view of our planet was a glimpse of
> divinity."[64]

God alone can ultimately satisfy the yearning of the human heart. But if we seek God with all our heart, we find God not only in our heart but in the vastness of creation; and the world in the heart of Christ. Far from having lost anything, we have found everything, and we can understand the truth of one mystic's celebration of no boundary.

> "Mine are the heavens and mine is the earth.
> Mine are the nations,
> the just are mine, and mine the sinners,
> and God himself is mine and for me,
> because Christ is mine and all for me."[65]

For this loving knowledge gives birth to wisdom that enlightens us with an inner spirit of discernment. Through the gentle stirring of the Spirit of love, our heart knows intuitively what we are to do in any concrete circumstance. In freedom of spirit we discover God's Spirit guiding us from within. Our prayer and our life become more integrated, like breathing in and breathing out. They take on the pulsating rhythm of the cosmic heartbeat centred in the heart of Christ. The Trinity is living in us. Christ, the Word of God, opens our heart to the freedom of truth. The Spirit is released into the flow of our life empowering us to relate in love. This love is at once our adoration of God and our compassion for every other human being.

Realising so intimate a presence of God at the heart of all things, Teilhard de Chardin could make this response to Jesus as the Christ of God.

> "Every presence makes me feel that you are near me;
> every touch is the touch of your hand;
> every necessity transmits to me
> the pulsation of your will.
> So true is this, that everything around me
> that is essential and enduring
> has become for me the dominance and, in some way,
> the substance of your heart.
> That is why it is impossible for me
> to look on your face without seeing in it
> the radiance of every reality and every goodness:
> your cosmic body."[66]

11.2 A Sign of the Presence of God

We have now completed our pilgrimage seeking and exploring a sign for the times. In discovering the heart of Christ at the heart of all reality, we have rediscovered our own heart and know it as a sacred space; a sign of God's presence in us and for us: a radiance of love. So we may complete Karl Rahner's reflection with which we opened this inner journey and review its movement from the heart of Christ to every human heart.

"What is invoked is that Heart
which is the innermost thing and the unifying thing;
the mystery which defies all analysis;
the silent law mightier than any organization.
What is named is that place in which
the mystery of man opens into the mystery of God;
empty infinity, becoming aware of itself,
calls out to God's infinite fullness.

It is the pierced Heart that is invoked,
the anguished, exhausted Heart,
the Heart that has died.
That which is named here signifies love,
the love that is unthinkable and selfless,
the love that conquers in utter failure,
that triumphs when it is powerless,
that gives life when it is killed;
the love that is God.

This word proclaims that God is near
to the one who prays.
It speaks of what is utterly bodily
and yet is all in all,
so that we can count the heartbeats and know,
weeping for joy, that we need go no further,
for we have found God.

Is it possible to deny
that what we encounter in this word
is ourselves, our present destiny,
and the real meaning of being a Christian,
something that is laid upon us, a burden
but also a grace, entrusted to us as a mission?

God's eternal Word,
sprung from the heart of the Father,
has sought out our own heart,
suffered it to the end, and will keep it for ever.

The Heart of Jesus is a name for that reality
in which the nameless mystery, whom we call God,
is present, not as mysteriously withholding himself,
but as self-giving intimacy: present where we are,
in the central source of our earthly being,
the heart."[67]

11.3 Making a Mandala

When we have experienced the renewing process of an
inner journey of faith, however, we usually feel the need to
try and encapsulate what it has meant for us. Making a
mandala is one practical and creative way of doing this. In
it we image our thanksgiving for what we have discovered
by reflecting upon our own life story in relation to the faith
that has inspired us. There are many ways of approaching
this exercise. The one suggested here relates to the process
explored in our pilgrimage to the heart and is inspired by
the contemplation to attain the love of God with which
Ignatius of Loyola concludes his *Spiritual Exercises*.[68]

The simplest way to begin is by making a circle and
dividing it into four by means of a cross sign. Draw round
the point of intersection of the vertical and horizontal lines
a small centre circle. Work within the control of this simple
structure. It can be amazing and encouraging to see the
spiritual creativity it can engender as we try to image how
our contemplation has led us into communion with God
and all creation. The whole process of making the mandala
is open to prayer as we let the Spirit guide us through our
memory and reflection.

The outer circle reminds us of the cosmic dimension of
reality as well as the everyday life of the world held in
God's providential love. We use all the images provided by
creation to express our inner spiritual world. To colours,
shapes and patterns we may add words or texts to clarify
our meaning.

In the first segment of the circle we express our thanksgiving for all the gifts of life and creativity that we have received. In particular, we remember the forgiveness, healing and growth that has set us free from all that holds us back in our past.

In the second segment of the circle we express thanksgiving for God's presence within all creation and that in Christ God is so close to us in our earthly life. More particularly, we remember our own personal call setting us free to share in the mission of Christ on earth in the service of others.

In the third segment of the circle we express our thanksgiving for the way in which God has laboured for us in all creation at every stage of its evolution, and Christ has suffered for us and strengthened us through his passion. In particular, we remember the suffering and diminishments of our own life not only as negatives but as opportunities to grow in compassion.

In the fourth segment of the circle we express thanksgiving for God's transcendence, the wonder of reality that draws us onward in our journey to further growth and showers us with surprise blessings. In particular, we remember the Spirit of the risen Christ in our joys; and all that has brought us peace; along with the new life that comes after pain in our lives.

Then we look at our small centre circle: the sacred space of the heart. This is our own personal space for God at the heart of all things. We may like to leave it symbolically empty or we may find in an image a way of making this a symbol of God's space. This is the heart of our thanksgiving.

Later we may find that we want to integrate still further the images of the different segments of our mandala. This is a natural progression as the patterns of light and shadow interconnect and relate, imaging the reconciliation of opposites. We let the mandala change and grow, reflecting our own change and growth: we let the wheel turn.[69]

An imaginative vision of the Trinity looking on the world as if from outer space using two mandala images: Andre Rublev's fifteenth century Russian icon of the Old Testament Trinity (Tretjakov Gallery, Moscow) and NASA photo of planet earth.

11.4 The World is a Mandala

Our pilgrimage at an end, we return to the mandala as a symbol of the process of the journey. It has led us, like a map, to the heart of reality in ourselves and in the world, only now we have explored its power to centre as it unifies and to radiate as it releases. The light shining through the mandala of the great rose window in Chartres cathedral has illuminated the labyrinth of our journey. Faith has given us God's vision of the world and the mission to earth it.

Now, as if from outer space, we can look upon our world, remembering creation by name: its lands, its peoples, its overwhelming beauty and complex power. This is the world God loved so much, and God is at its heart. Everything speaks of God simply by its appearing. But it also speaks of what we have done with our planet both for the development of its resources and for its pollution and pain. The world itself with its shadow and light as a sphere of teeming life and woundedness, is now our mandala. But from the timeless perspective of faith and in the reconciling love of God, we see primarily, like the astronaut from outer space, its most amazing beauty: the radiance that is the glory of God.

In his contemplation on the Incarnation, Ignatius of Loyola depicts the Trinity of God looking with compassion upon the world as though from outer space.[70] We could image a scene with two contrasting mandalas: a view of our planet from outer space, such as NASA gives us, being looked upon by André Rublev's fifteenth century Russian icon of the Trinity. In the icon, the three persons of the Trinity form a circle round the table of the Eucharist where their gaze rests. But the circle of their communion is open to the world: an invitation to all creation to enter into the loving relationship of the Trinity. The two mandalas thus image relationship between God and the world in personal terms. That is their value.

The integral and radical presence of God at the heart of all creation, however, suggests only one mandala in which the world, like a global monstrance, reveals through the cosmic radiance of love, that the heart is a sacred space.

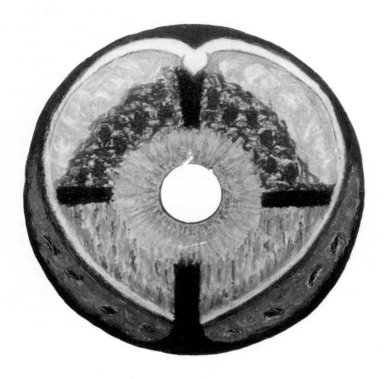

The globe of the world, visible now in the mandala symbol, can centre our gaze in a mode of contemplation that holds us open to the Trinity of God present in creation. At the edge of a circle of wholeness is the Spirit hovering, the dove of peace, heart-shaped, holding in a gesture of love all that needs reconciling in the world. Within the expanse of the globe, Christ, in all creation, manifests God in a creative tension of opposites symbolised by the tree of the cross. But at the unifying centre of the mandala is the still point of the world: the sacred space of the heart where God, the ground of all being and the root of our relatedness, is open to the world and the

world to God. From this centre is released, like rays from
the sun, the cosmic radiance of love that creates communion. This communion is symbolised in the wheat and the
vine that creation, held between sea and sky, provides for
its own transformation into Christ.

11.5 The Heart is a Sacred Space

Circling now is love,
a pure white dove, spiralling
in cosmic rhythm, the Spirit
folding in on earth:
a jewel in rainbow hue,
deep, the deepest blue
ultramarine of seas, specked
with silver scale in buoyant oceans;
floods of water flowing,
mirroring not knowing,
deep that calls on deep
while humanity's asleep,
the darkened shade of night
where shadows fall.

But dawn breaks out in light,
a light blue, cloud-shaped,
flocking the floating sky,
holding the spreading air
there, where green grows gold
in fields of wheat and rye
and gold grows green with leaf
as every tree grows, who knows
how high in hovering sky
that cherishes such life
in forests dark where earthy foot
falls and moves as yet unseen
while winged flight sings out its song,
a yearning, crying Lord, how long?

For there, where sturdy oak
rooted deep in loam rich earth,
meets slender sinewy vine
and feeling tendrils touch
and hold strong branching arms,
is communion
of peoples, planets, stars and streams
shining in translucent host
and deep red, grape-pressed wine,
as with gold and fiery glow
the sun radiates
the love of hearth and home
and centres life around a space,
God's own.

Now earth too can hear the cry,
no louder than a sigh, breathing,
the Spirit that creates a hush,
as strong the heartbeat pounds
in silence still that sounds
the Word echoing.
Deep so deep it falls,
earth adoring to the ground.
Yet still no sound is heard,
only a heartbeat centres there the world:
the Trinity in oneness closely bound,
has no boundary, for still
the Heart is a Sacred Space
where God is found.

11.6 Living from the Centre

What remains for us now is an ongoing process encouraged by the hope we have been given. This does not mean
that we cease to struggle with our own particular version of
humanity. We remain ourselves with our own temperament
and character. This is the challenge that is personally ours

as the adventure of being alive. But we can help ourselves by making a regular review of our response to God in our own life's experience so that we are living in touch with our own centre. Basically we go on asking: "Does what I am doing now resonate with the truth of who I am? Does it reflect the identity I have imaged in my own mandala?" We can express this review in terms of five R's.

REST in an awareness of the presence of God: the Blessed Trinity. Let this be a time of thanksgiving for life, light and love. In our world of pressure, haste and noise, it is vital that we take time off for prayer and reflection, and that it should be associated with a time for rest, relaxation and renewal of body, mind and heart. Now is the time to find a restful posture and to focus on our breathing for a while so that we can be open to God's presence within our heart. This rest can relate us to the centre of our mandala.

REMEMBER our life in the context of God's word to us in Scripture. Let our experience, all that has happened to us today, just come into our consciousness. God accepts us, the whole of us, just as we are. Now we must do the same: accept the whole of our life. Non-acceptance will block the way to growth. Only the real person consciously accepted can be transformed into a reflection of Christ in our own unique and personal way. This is a healing of our memories as it is also a remembering of the Christ way of being and doing. This remembering can relate us to the first segment of our mandala.

REFLECT upon our own personal call as we have discovered it during times of peace and harmony when we understood how we could be truly ourselves. Then ask the Holy Spirit to shed light upon our day's experience so that we can discern how it measures up to what we already know is our Christ-centred self. Allow the beam of light to focus on one area which surfaces into consciousness now. We are bringing together Christ's values and what actually happens in our life. What kind of response is being asked of us now? This reflection can relate us to the second segment of our mandala.

RETURN to God as the love and mercy of God draws us now in forgiveness and healing. Repent of all that seems to fall short of Christ's way for us now. Remain in the sense of intimacy that comes from recognising the wounds in our own heart, and in finding new life and hope through the wound in Christ's heart. This re-turning to God will have its own distinctive colour and atmosphere depending upon each day's experience. This re-turning can relate us to the third segment of our mandala.

RESOLVE to begin again in the way Christ has shown us. Renew ourselves for the mission and ministry given to us by God to be with Christ and empowered by the Holy Spirit. Re-orientate our life in a practical way so that we can realise in our everyday life the vision we see. This resolve towards the future helps to integrate our time of prayer, reflection and renewal with the life we live during the rest of the day, and energises us for the involvement and work it entails. This resolve can relate us to the fourth segment of our mandala.

We end by returning to our Rest, simply allowing ourselves to be loved by God so that we too may love.

"In returning and rest you shall be saved."

(Isaiah 30:15)

This exercise follows the same kind of process that would happen if we were to visit a trusted friend in order to reflect seriously upon the way in which our life was proceeding. We would begin by sitting down and relaxing together with the real courtesy of grateful thanks. The greater the intimacy the more relaxed we would be and the easier the lapses into silence and quiet. Then the memories would come about what had happened since our last meeting. Together we would reflect upon their meaning and value in the light of past experience. If the relationship had suffered in any way we would restore it. If all was well, we would strengthen it with signs of affection and shared hopes and plans. Finally we would prepare for future action and meeting in whatever way seemed most realistic and capable of encouraging the relationship and the mission to be accomplished.

The five points indicate a process of review, but each is a mode of prayer and reflection on its own. The amount of time given to each point on any given day depends upon the individual person and the nature of the day's experience. What genuinely helps us, is the guideline for its application. As always, we need both freedom of spirit and the discipline of a disciple! But such a process renewed regularly, allows us to keep in constant touch with the presence of God within us and to become ever more conscious of the wisdom of the heart. In this way we can discern all that happens to us in the light of what we have come to know is our own personal vocation. This is the personal responsibility of each one of us. No one else can live our life for us. It is God's unique gift to every person to live![71]

Notes

1. Chandogya Upanishad, 8.1. *The Upanishads*, p. 121. Penguin Books, 1965.

2. See R. Wilhelm and C. G. Jung, *The Secret of the Golden Flower*, pp. 81-136. Routledge and Kegan Paul, 1962; and C.G. Jung, *Collected Works*, Vol. 9. Part 1, p. 357 and pp. 355-390. Routledge and Kegan Paul, 1959.

3. Karl Rahner, *Christian in the Market Place*, p. 111. Sheed and Ward, 1966. For background to Chapter 1 on the heart as a primordial symbol, see K. Rahner's Theological Investigations 3, pp. 321-330. Darton, Longman and Todd, 1967.

4. Julian of Norwich, *Showings*, Chapter 4, p. 181. Paulist Press, New York, 1978.

5. See Bernard McGinn's clear exposition of Eckhart's distinctive teaching on the Godhead and creation in his introduction to Meister Eckhart, *The Essential Sermons, Commentaries, Treatises and Defence*; pp. 30-57. Paulist Press, New York, 1981. In this context, I would also like to acknowledge my debt to the writing of Raimundo Pannikar. See *The Trinity and the Religious Experience of Man*. Darton, Longman and Todd, 1973; and *The Silence of God*. Orbis Books, 1989.

6. See C. G. Jung, *op. cit.* Vol. 11, p. 156. Routledge and Kegan Paul, 1958.

7. See *Dictionary of the English Language*, p. 1881. Longman, 1991. There are many forms of yoga in the Eastern tradition, but for a discussion relevant to this context, including the use of *The Spiritual Exercises of St. Ignatius*, see *Yoga and the West*; in C. G. Jung, *op. cit.* Vol. 11, pp. 529-537. The link between the spiritual 'soul' and the 'psyche', relevant throughout this reflection is highlighted in this Gospel text as the English 'soul' translates the Greek 'psyche'. For more on the relationship between spiritual guidance and psychotherapy, see article: *Spiritual Direction and Counselling/Therapy* by Mary Grant and Pamela Hayes; in *The Way Supplement 69*, Autumn 1990.

8. R. Wilhelm and C. G. Jung, *op. cit.* p. 93.

9. John of the Cross, *The Ascent of Mount Carmel*, 1.13.11; in *The Collected Works of St John of the Cross*, p. 104. I.C.S. Publications, Washington D.C., 1979.

10. C.G. Jung, *op. cit.* Vol. 11, p. 158, note 9.

11. For a brief background to both kinds of meditation, see *The Prayer of the Heart: East and West*, Pamela Hayes; in *One in 2000*? Paul McPartlan, pp. 89-100. St. Pauls, 1993.

12. See *Dictionary of the English Language* p. 344 *op. cit.* The word 'contemplation' bears the idea of a penetrating look upon a space deemed sacred like a temple.

13. See John of the Cross, *The Ascent of Mount Carmel* 2.22.5, *op. cit.* p. 180.

14. See Anon., *The Cloud of Unknowing*, Chapters 6-7, pp. 130-134. Paulist Press, New York, 1981.

15. See inspiring short study of Herbert Alphonso, *The Personal Vocation*, C.I.S. Rome, 1990.

16. See as an accessible beginning on dreams, C. G. Jung, *Memories, Dreams and Reflections*. Collins Fontana, 1967.

17. I owe this story to its use by W. Jaffe in *Liberating the Heart*, p. 46. Inner City Books, Toronto, Canada, 1990.

18. See C. G. Jung, *op. cit.* Vol. 11, p. 157.

19. See for example, *Meister Eckhart: Sermons and Treatises*, Edited by M.O'C. Walshe, Vol. 1, p. 1. Element, 1979. Eckhart is referring to Augustine of Hippo's question. For a helpful exposition of the birth image, see Oliver Davies, *Meister Eckhart: Mystical Theologian*, pp. 126-159. S.P.C.K., 1991.

20. See on the relation between the mystics and existentialists, William Johnston's relevant introduction to his edition of *The Cloud of Unknowing and Book of Privy Counselling*, pp. 10-16. Doubleday, Image Books, 1973.

21. See Teresa of Avila, *The Interior Castle* 5.1.11, p. 90. Paulist Press, New York, 1979.

22. For insights on the relationship between Teresa of Avila and John of the Cross, see E. W. Truman Dicken, *The Imagery of the Interior Castle and its Implications*; in *Ephemerides Carmeliticae* XXI pp. 211-218. I.C.S. Rome, 1970.

23. See John of the Cross, *The Living Flame of Love*: poem, stanza 1; and commentary 1:1-13; in *op. cit.* pp. 579-584

24. See Teresa of Avila, *op. cit.* 5.1.8, 11. pp. 89-90.

25. Ibid. 7.1.6,7. p. 175; and 1.2.8, p. 42.

26. I am grateful for this fragment MS Douce 262ff. 132v.-134v., given to me by James Walsh S.J. while he was translating it for publication. It is now available in the appendix of *The Pursuit of Wisdom*, pp. 297-298. Paulist Press, New York, 1988. See also for an example of a parallel passage in Julian of Norwich, *op. cit.* Chapter 68, pp. 312-313, where Julian speaks of her soul being in the midst of her heart. She also speaks in this context, like Teresa of Avila, of spaciousness within the heart.

27. The same Greek word 'pneuma' is used in the New Testament for the English, 'spirit', 'wind' and 'breath'. See *Manual Greek Lexicon of the New Testament*, ed. G. Abbot-Smith, p. 367. T. and T. Clark, 1964.

28. The first verse of this poem was written by an unnamed friend of Rollo May who quotes it in a footnote on p. 135 in *The Courage to Create*. Collins, 1976. It inspired me to write the other two verses.

29. This last phrase, newly explored by Rupert Sheldrake in *The Rebirth of Nature*, pp. 62-64, Rider, London, 1991, demonstrates how much this section owes to the scientists who have made known the vision and trends of their research for the lay person. I am especially grateful to John Polkinghorne for his books like the trilogy: *One World*, 1986; *Science and Creation*, 1988; and *Science and Providence*, 1989; as well as to Arthur Peacocke for his *Creation and the World of Science*, 1979; and to Paul Davies for *The Cosmic Blueprint*, 1987. P. Teilhard de Chardin's books referred to here are: *The Phenomenon of Man*, 1959; and *Le Milieu Divin*, 1968.

30. See C. G. Jung, *op. cit.* Vol.11, p. 187 and p. 419.

31. See Ken Wilber, *No Boundary*, pp. 38-41. Shambhala, 1985. I am indebted to the interdisciplinary exploration gathered together in this book from the author's more specialised works.

32. See John Polkinghorne, *Science and Creation.* S.P.C.K., 1988, p. 83, note 36; on David Bohm's *Wholeness and the Implicate Order*, p. 177. R.K.P., 1980. I am grateful for John Polkinghorne's comment on the passage in D. Bohm's work. It allowed me to relish the vision of wholeness without expecting it to be fully explanatory.

33. See Meister Eckhart, *op. cit.* pp. 39-44 for a summary of this aspect of Eckhart's teaching. For an introduction to Eckhart that is both scholarly and popular, see Cyprian Smith, *The Way of Paradox.* Darton, Longman and Todd, 1987.

34. P. Teilhard de Chardin, *The Heart of Matter*, pp. 43-44. Collins, 1978.

35. See Teilhard de Chardin, *Journal 6*, quoted by Robert Faricy in *The Spirituality of Teilhard de Chardin*, p. 19. Winston Press, Minneapolis, 1981.

36. See Hildegard of Bingen, *Book of Divine Works*, 4.11; in *Hildegard of Bingen: An Anthology*, ed. F. Bowie and O. Davies, p. 96. S.P.C.K., 1990.

37. John of the Cross, *The Spiritual Canticle*, stanzas 13,14, *op. cit.* p. 714.

38. I have drawn upon my article *Women and the Passion*; in *The Way Supplement 58*, Spring 1987, pp. 65-73, for this section on Mary Magdalene. For this purpose I have assumed the long tradition which tends to equate her with the woman who was a sinner in Luke 7:36-50, without analysing it critically.

39. See for Gregory of Nyssa's teaching on perpetual progress, *From Glory*

to Glory: Texts from Gregory of Nyssa, ed. J. Danielou and H. Musurillo, pp. 47-71 and pp. 196-197. John Murray, London, 1962.

40. See Ibid. pp. 261-262. This passage which remains a key to Gregory of Nyssa's teaching, is also accessible in the introduction to his *The Life of Moses*, pp. 21-22. Paulist Press, New York, 1978.

41. *Constitutions of the Society of the Sacred Heart*, p. 70, nn. 20, 21. Rome, 1987.

42. See T. S. Eliot, *East Coker*; in *Four Quartets*, p. 28. Faber, 1944.

43. See *A Letter of Private Direction* in Anon. *The Pursuit of Wisdom*, p. 244. Paulist Press, New York, 1988.

44. See Julian of Norwich, *op. cit.* pp. 322-323.

45. See Brant Pelphrey, *Christ Our Mother*, pp. 25-33. D.L.T., 1989. The section on the theology of kindness in his introduction highlights what is in Julian's text.

46. See Julian of Norwich, *The Revelations of Divine Love*, edited by James Walsh, pp. 33-37 and pp. 144-171. Anthony Clarke, 1973. This translation captures the original play on language and its theological implications.

47. See Marie-Louise Von Franz, in *The Way of the Dream*, p. 299. Toronto, 1988.

48. See poem *Turning Point*; in *Selected Poetry of Rainer Maria Rilke*, ed. Stephen Mitchell, p. 133. Picador Pan Books, London, 1987.

49. Rainer Maria Rilke, *Letters to a Young Poet*, ed. Stephen Mitchell, pp. 76-78. Vintage, New York, 1986.

50. Antoine de Saint-Exupéry, *The Little Prince*, pp. 66-72. Piccolo Pan Books, 1974.

51. I am very grateful to April O'Leary for allowing me to use her unpublished poem.

52. P. Teilhard de Chardin, *The Evolution of Chastity*; in *Towards the Future*, pp. 85-87. Collins, 1974.

53. P. Teilhard de Chardin, *The Mystical Milieu*; in *Writings in Time of War*, pp. 117-118, 120. Collins, 1968.

54. Taylor Wang (China / U.S.A.) in *The Home Planet*, ed. Kevin W. Kelley, p. 60. Addison Wesley, 1988.

55. Pham Tuan (Vietnam) Ibid., p. 85.

56. Sigmund Jähn (G.D.R.) Ibid., p. 141.

57. Boris Volynov (U.S.S.R.) Ibid., p. 88.

58. Oleg At'kov (U.S.S.R.) Ibid., p. 117.

59. Muhammad Ahmad Faris (Syria) Ibid., p. 76.

60. Sultan Bin Salman al-Saud (Saudi Arabia) Ibid., p. 82.

61. Edgar Mitchell (U.S.A.) Ibid., p. 138.

62. John-David Bartoe (U.S.A.) Ibid., p. 85.

63. Janet Erskine Stuart *Poems*, p. 25. Longmans, 1924.

64. Edgar Mitchell in *The Home Planet, op. cit.* p. 52

65. John of the Cross, *op. cit.* p. 669

66. P. Teilhard de Chardin *The Mystical Milieu*; in *op. cit.* p. 146

67. Karl Rahner, *op. cit.* pp. 111-112, 115

68. See *Contemplation to Attain the Love of God*, in *The Spiritual Exercises of St Ignatius*, ed. L. Puhl nn. 230-237, pp. 101-103. Loyola University Press Chicago, 1951.

69. Apart from references made to C. G. Jung in note 1., the following books are helpful on making mandalas: Susanne F. Fincher, *Creating Mandalas*, Shambhala, 1991; Jose and Miriam Arguelles, *Mandala*, Shambhala, 1985.

70. See *The Spiritual Exercises of St Ignatius, op. cit.* nn. 102-109, pp. 49-51.

71. For background to the review, see George Ashenbrenner on *Consciousness Examen*; in *Notes on the Spiritual Exercises of St Ignatius Loyola.* ed. David L. Fleming, pp. 175-185. St. Louis, 1981.